The BENJAMIN Blessing

God's five-fold plan for your destiny

Pastor Rick Hawkins

Family Praise Center
San Antonio, Texas

Copyright © 2002—Rick Hawkins

ISBN 1-932007-00-8

Pastor Rick Hawkins
P.O. Box 28402
San Antonio, TX 78228

Produced by HonorNet

ACKNOWLEDGEMENTS

To my Savior and Lord, Jesus Christ, without whom I am naught. For His patience with me and for His guidance throughout this project and every aspect of life.

To my wife, Robin, who has loved patiently and withstood much over the years…and to our three beautiful children, who are the treasure of my posterity. Dustin, Crystal, and Kendra—I love you all and pray that the life I've lived will influence you to excel beyond anything I've dared to dream for you.

To the church I pastor, *Family Praise Center of San Antonio, Texas.* That God has chosen to send such wonderful people with such a wealth of talent and treasure overwhelms me. Thank you for being the fulfillment of God's plan for my life in San Antonio, Texas.

To my pastor, Bishop Gary McIntosh. We've walked this road for more than 25 years. Thank you for your continual counsel.

To my assistant, Dori. You are a transcriptionist (that word was created for you). *Write the book, I say!*

To a network of friends and associates who have encouraged this project and who believe in the message. To the *Knights*—success to you and success to the kingdom of God.

I am deeply grateful for the research, writing, and editing of Mary Ellen Breitwiser, Jim Kerby, and Norma Collins, who assisted me with the presentation of this life-changing message for those living in the last pivotal moments before Jesus' return.

Jake Jones, thanks for the connection, man! You believed in this project the moment you saw it.

CONTENTS

FOREWORD

The Old Testament is filled with types and shadows of things to come in the New Testament. For instance, Joshua, whose Hebrew name, *Yeshua,* means, "The Lord is salvation," was a type of Jesus Christ, the Savior of the New Testament church.

In Pastor Rick Hawkins' new book, *The Benjamin Blessing,* you will see the many ways in which Benjamin, the youngest son of Jacob, was a type and shadow throughout the Old Testament of the church of the new millennium. I believe that as you read this book, you will see how you can relate to some of the things that Benjamin went through and how, just as Benjamin ended up receiving many blessings from his brother Joseph, God has abundant blessings in store for you.

Reading *The Benjamin Blessing* will inspire you to move out of the land of just enough to the land of more than enough. This book is thought provoking and exciting. It will challenge you to step up to your place of authority as a child of God and awaken the Benjamin in you.

Randy Morrison, Pastor
Speak the Word Church,
Minneapolis, MN

PREFACE

Do these names mean anything to you? Ehud, Mordecai, Jonathan, Saul, Mephibosheth, Esther, Paul, Ithai. These are people who influenced change in their generation. They are referred to in Scripture as Benjamites.

The life of ambiguous wandering and mediocre meandering must come to a halt for the people of God. This is an hour when the plan and purpose of God for your personal life must be paramount, and it must preempt all other suggested avenues of fulfillment.

We have arrived at a time in history that requires a studious people to remain focused on the mandate of God for the church.

Many societal and generational transitions have taken place in the last century, and each change brought with it responsibility for the people of God. The equipping agency for God's people has been and always will be the church—a five-fold empowerment company that is designed for the purpose of supplying the equipment necessary to affect change in that generation. Ephesians 4:12 describes the church as a complex organism, listing the fundamental requisites for proper function—a *five*-fold gift. First, there is the apostle, then the prophet, evangelist, teacher, and last, the pastor.

Notice the order of the list with the apostle being first. In Paul's letter to the church at Corinth (1 Corinthians 12:28), he states again that God has set the apostle first. Jesus made an interesting statement concerning *firsts*. Both Matthew 19:30 and Mark 10:31 record Jesus saying, *But many who are first will be last, and many who are last will be first.*

The life of Benjamin reflects this last-shall-be-first syndrome. When reconciled to his brother Joseph, who had been sent ahead by God to preserve a remnant unto Himself, it was Benjamin, the last-born, who was seated at the foot of the table. Being last established his position at the end. It was there that Benjamin received from the hand of his predecessor, Joseph, a five-fold blessing that would distinguish him from his brothers.

With the apostle always being listed first, is it any wonder that it would be the last office to receive proper recognition today?

As these last days of the church thrust toward their inevitable conclusion, the subject of the apostle is being discussed more than ever before. And we must remember that it was the last apostle to join the twelve who were personally appointed by Jesus—a radical Benjamite named Paul—who changed the course of the Christian faith and civilization itself by writing two-thirds of the New Testament in the form of letters dashed off to his "problem" churches or to friends who needed his advice.

The Benjamin blessing is coming your way, and it has an anointing that sets you apart—a five-fold equipping that will take you from last to first. The Greek rendering of the word *first* is "proton"—a positive force. And it is with positive optimism that Benjamin steps to the forefront with a declaration, "Follow me as I follow Christ."

As you embark on this journey through the life of Benjamin, get ready to receive your five-fold blessing.

> *It was he* [Christ] *who gave some to be apostles, some to be prophets, some to be evangelists, and some to be pastors and teachers, to prepare God's people for works of service, so that the body of Christ may be built up until we all reach unity in the faith and in the knowledge of the Son of God and become mature, attaining to the whole measure of the fullness of Christ.*
> —Ephesians 4:12

The Benjamin Blessing

I am a part of the Benjamin Blessing.

I was born for such a time as this.

My future is secure and my present makes sense.

I have purpose and potential.

My steps are ordered.

I am destined to succeed.

I do not need popularity, position, or promotion.

I live by prayer.

I labor with power.

I cannot be bought or compromised.

I am responsible for my own actions.

I produce excellence by my own attitude.

I now receive my five-fold Benjamin Blessing.

This is my generation.

It was waiting for me to arrive.

I am here, and things will never be the same!

1

Benjamin's Heritage

As he looked about and saw his brother Benjamin, his own mother's son, he asked, "Is this your youngest brother, the one you told me about?" And he said, "God be gracious to you, my son." Deeply moved at the sight of his brother, Joseph hurried out and looked for a place to weep. He went into his private room and wept there. After he had washed his face, he came out and, controlling himself, said, "Serve the food."...The men had been seated before him in the order of their ages, from the firstborn to the youngest; and they looked at each other in astonishment. When portions were served to them from Joseph's table, Benjamin's portion was five times as much as anyone else's....

To all of them he gave each man changes of raiment; but to Benjamin he gave three hundred pieces of silver, and five changes of raiment.

—Genesis 43:29-31,33,34 NIV; 45:22 KJV

Surely these verses offer a brief glimpse of a pivotal page from one of the most moving and poignant dramas ever recorded in the history of mankind.

Twelve Hebrew brothers are reunited, not in the familiar hills and meadows of their beloved homeland, but in the capital of Egypt, the proud and powerful enemy and haughty and harsh oppressor of much of the known world, who especially despised their ancestors. Indeed, on this prophetic occasion, the eleven sons of Jacob have been seated at their own table, away from Joseph, governor of Egypt, second only to the Pharaoh. His Egyptian aides and staff are also seated separately ...*because Egyptians could not eat with Hebrews, for that is detestable to Egyptians* (Genesis 43:32).

Joseph was also their "lost" brother whom they did not yet recognize.

Thirteen years before, the ten older brothers had grown jealous and resentful of their father's teenaged favorite who traipsed around in a wonderful "technicolor" coat. Joseph also aggravated them by cockily relating his dreams, outlandish scenarios in which he was the supreme hero of the family, with his brothers (even his father) bowing and recognizing his dominance.

You remember the story—how one day Joseph was sent to check on his brothers in the fields. When they saw him coming, their resentment boiled and they plotted his death in the desert. But brother Reuben pleaded for the lad's life, and brother Judah devised an alternate plan to sell the dreamer to a passing merchant caravan headed for Egypt.

Joseph's coat of many colors, soaked in an animal's blood, convinced Jacob that his beloved son was dead. So the brothers were rid of the sibling they despised, and must have smugly wondered how the boy who dreamed of ruling others would fare as a slave to the Egyptians.

"GOD SENT ME AHEAD OF YOU TO PRESERVE...A REMNANT ON EARTH..."

How could they possibly have known that their treachery, meant for evil, would trigger the next phase of God's plan and bring about good, ultimately including even their own deliverance. The events to follow would change the destiny of not just their family but also of the end-time church ordained to restore victory and blessing to God's people in the last days of time. They had no idea that their evil deeds had set the stage for a great deliverance—in Joseph's words: *...God sent me ahead of you to preserve...**a remnant on earth...*** (Genesis 45:7).

Catch a glimpse of the divine irony that causes a once-proud patriarch, now fallen on hard times, to send his traitorous sons into the land of his people's traditional enemy to beg for food. In Egypt they encounter the ruling governor, a former dreamer elevated to power as a result of being able to interpret the Pharaoh's God-given dreams and implement preparations for the coming famine.

But wait, that's not all. The governor turns out to be the patriarch's long-lost and lamented son, sold into slavery by his brothers. And rather than being vengeful and vindictive, Joseph forgives his brothers, is reunited with his father, and brings his entire extended family under his protection and provision in Egypt.

But if you've read the Book, you certainly are aware that, unfortunately, everybody *didn't* live happily ever after. Yes, the closing days of Jacob's life were eventful and significant. But he died without realizing God's ultimate promise and plan.

Joseph certainly played a major role in the sensational saga of God's chosen people. But his illustrious life came to an end, his personal dreams fulfilled, but not the final realization of God's prophetic plan.

Before dying, even as Jacob bestowed a blessing upon each of his twelve sons—from the first-born Reuben to each child of his wives, Leah and Rachel, and his concubines, Bilhah and Zilpah— his words foretold an outline of events that would shape the history of the church and foreshadow its eternal destiny. Each of Joseph's brothers had personality traits relevant to the church in this hour.

The rest of the story

Which brings us to the significant part of the story. The special attention, blessing, and provision directed to Benjamin, the youngest, in the Genesis account is not simply a curious anomaly. The story of how and why he got his name, the prophetic blessing of his dying father, and the bestowment of five times the resources given to his brothers is highly significant, as we shall see.

...THE BESTOW-MENT OF FIVE TIMES THE RESOURCES GIVEN TO HIS BROTHERS IS HIGHLY SIGNIFICANT.

Just as the histories of the tribes descended from Jacob's other eleven sons provide a remarkable picture of the church up to our day, so the story of the last-born Benjamin provides insight to the last-day church. As we take a closer look at this remarkable account, I believe you will recognize a significant end-time group of people best described as the Benjamite church.

This group of believers has been given a special mission, and finds itself in the midst of unprecedented circumstances. This church will enjoy a special relationship to the Father...and will go forth to carry out His purpose and plan with a five-fold blessing and five-fold provision to equip it for the challenges of the final hour before the second coming of Christ.

I believe we are stepping up to this greatest move of God the earth has ever experienced right now, and it carries with it an anointing so positive that it is magnetic in its appeal and attraction. I refer to 1 Corinthians 12:28, a catalog of spiritual gifts, listing ...*first of all apostles, second prophets, third teachers, then workers of miracles, also those having gifts of healing, those able to help others, those with gifts of administration, and those speaking in different kinds of tongues.*

Remember Jesus said the last shall be first (Matthew 19:30; Mark 10:31). I call it the reverse order of restoration. With this in mind, the first gift that God released in this century was the gift of tongues in 1906 at the Azusa Street Revival in Los Angeles. From tongues, there was a transition into denominationalism—an attempt to organize (the gift of administration) all the broadly based Pentecostal efforts birthed at Azusa Street.

From there we went to helping others with a great missions movement that led to the healing move of God in the late 1940s with Oral Roberts and miracles. With the '60s and '70s came the Jesus People movement. It stripped the gospel message to bare essentials, the chief tenet being that Jesus is the "one way" to God. Out of this movement came those who were gifted to teach.

The '80s and '90s were ushered in by the prophets. "Get ready! Get ready! Get ready!" T.D. Jakes shouted. The prophet always precedes the apostle. The apostolic anointing hasn't been emphasized until now, and this is no accident. Paul said the apostle will emerge from the tribe of Benjamin.

What does this have to do with you? I believe that as you look into God's Word with fresh vision…as you reach out to the Father with a new longing and desire for His presence…as you recommit your love for Jesus and your calling to His Great Commission with all your heart and soul and mind…as you look with new clarity and understanding through the eyes of the Holy Spirit—you will cry out with a new passion that lifts your very being into a whole new realm of spirit and reality:

"O God, my God, I am a Benjamite!"

2

The Blessing

When portions were served to them [the brothers] *from Joseph's table, Benjamin's portion was five times as much as anyone else's. So they feasted and drank freely with him.*

To each of them he gave new clothing, but to Benjamin he gave three hundred shekels of silver and five sets of clothes.

—Genesis 43:34; 45:22

In their best-selling book, *The Blessing*, Gary Smalley and Dr. John Trent relate the Old Testament tradition of imparting upon each child in a family an individual blessing, using descriptive word pictures as well as a special blessing for the firstborn. It is a custom still observed in Jewish families today.

I can see Jacob as he realizes he is at the end of his life. He says, "Bring the boys in. I'm old and ready to pass on. Line them up, it's time for me to prophesy."

This story reminds me so much of what my own father did the day before he passed away. He told my mom, "Bring all the kids in." I recognize this scene—I've been here.

In the last hours of his life, my father spoke with his children. He started with the oldest, my sister Connie; then Jo, Gloria, Doug, Randy, and me. He said to me, "Ricky, I'm so proud of you. Don't disappoint me. You preach the gospel all over the world. Son, your ministry just got started."

So I can visualize Jacob saying, "Bring the boys in here." I almost feel like I was there when it happened! He started with

Rueben, moved on to Simeon, Gad, Naphtali, Dan, Zebulun…on down the line until he got to the youngest. He looked at him and said, "Benjamin, you are a ravenous wolf. In the morning you'll devour the prey. At night you'll divide the spoil. Son, you have a hunting spirit."

Although Old Testament law prohibited arbitrarily bypassing the eldest son to give the firstborn's blessing to another child, it could and did happen from time to time—and it is particularly noted in Jacob's family.

Jacob's firstborn son was Reuben. Of him, Jacob said, *"…you are my firstborn, my might, the first sign of my strength, excelling in honor, excelling in power. Turbulent as the waters, you will no longer excel, for you went up onto your father's bed, onto my couch and defiled it"* (Genesis 49:3,4).

Interestingly enough, Reuben's grievous offense merits only one mention in one verse of the Genesis account. The verse says simply, *While Israel* [formerly Jacob] *was living in that region* [Migdal Eder], *Reuben went in and slept with his father's concubine Bilhah, and Israel heard of it* (Genesis 35:22). There is no record of how the problem was resolved—we know that Reuben continued to be a close part of the family. But he had squandered his birthright, and when it was time to receive his father's blessing as the firstborn, he received the long-deferred judgment.

Joseph, son number eleven, received the firstborn's blessing. Between Reuben and Joseph, however, nine sons were born.

Sons two and three—Simeon and Levi—were also cursed instead of blessed. *"…their swords are weapons of violence,"* said *Jacob. "Let me not enter their council, let me not join their assembly, for they have killed men in their anger and hamstrung oxen as they pleased. Cursed be their anger, so fierce, and their fury, so cruel! I will scatter them…and disperse them in Israel"* (Genesis 49:5-7).

Then there is Judah. Of him, Jacob said, *"...your brothers will praise you; your hand will be on the neck of your enemies; your father's sons will bow down to you. You are a lion's cub, O Judah; you return from the prey, my son. Like a lion he crouches and lies down, like a lioness—who dares to rouse him? The scepter will not depart from Judah, nor the ruler's staff from between his feet, until he comes to whom it belongs and the obedience of the nations is his. He will tether his donkey to a vine, his colt to the choicest branch; he will wash his garments in wine, his robes in the blood of grapes. His eyes will be darker than wine, his teeth whiter than milk"* (vv.8-12). From Judah's tribe came the Savior of the world.

Jacob prophesied that Zebulun would *"...live by the seashore and become a haven for ships; his border will extend toward Sidon"* (v.13). He told Issachar he was *"...a rawboned donkey lying down between two saddlebags. When he sees how good is his resting place and how pleasant is his land, he will bend his shoulder to the burden and submit to forced labor"* (vv.14,15).

Jacob continued his roll call of blessings—*"Dan will provide justice for his people as one of the tribes of Israel. Dan will be a serpent by the roadside, a viper along the path, that bites the horse's heels so that its rider tumbles backward"* (vv.16,17).

There is Gad, the "invader, armed and prepared." Jacob's words over him were, *"Gad will be attacked by a band of raiders, but he will attack them at their heels"* (v.19). He said *"Asher's food will be rich; he will provide delicacies fit for a king"* (v.20).

Jacob pictured Naphtali as *"...a doe set free that bears beautiful fawns"* (v.21). Jacob painted a word picture of the artistic qualities this son possessed. Naphtali spoke and wrote beautiful words.

It was his eleventh son, Joseph, that Jacob called *"...a fruitful vine, a fruitful vine near a spring, whose branches climb over a wall. With bitterness archers attacked him; they shot at him with hostility. But his bow remained steady, his strong arms stayed lim-*

ber, because of the hand of the Mighty One of Jacob, because of the Shepherd, the Rock of Israel, because of your father's God, who helps you, because of the Almighty, who blesses you with blessings of the heavens above, blessings of the deep that lies below, blessings of the breast and womb. Your father's blessings are greater than the blessings of the ancient mountains, than the bounty of the age-old hills. Let all these rest on the head of Joseph, on the brow of the prince among his brothers" (vv.22-26).

> "...HIS NAME WILL
> BE BENJAMIN,
> WHICH MEANS 'SON
> OF MY RIGHT HAND,'
> AND HE WILL BE A
> PERSON OF GREAT
> AUTHORITY."

This word picture illustrated how Joseph's unfailing trust in the Lord resulted in his providing a place of refuge for his family. Jacob's word picture carried a similar message to one used about Jesus in Psalm 1:3—He is like a tree planted by streams of water, which yields its fruit in season and whose leaf does not wither. Whatever he does prospers.

Finally, there is Benjamin. At his birth, while she lay dying, his mother called him Ben-oni, meaning "son of my sorrow." But his father immediately stepped in, saying, "No! This child will not carry a name with such a painfully negative reminder of the suffering caused by his birth. His name will be Benjamin, which means 'son of my right hand,' and he will be a person of great authority." In his blessing of this last son, Jacob said, "Benjamin is a ravenous wolf; in the morning he devours the prey, in the evening he divides the plunder" (v.27).

The personality of Benjamin

The appetite of a wolf is never truly satisfied. A wolf can eat seven times his weight in one day and still not be full. Webster defines the root word raven as "to take by force; to consume greedily; devour; to seek or seize as prey or plunder." Jacob was saying,

"Boy, you're a born pursuer. You're going to hunt, and you'll never be full. You'll war in the morning and celebrate at night. You will pursue in the daytime and praise in the nighttime."

When I began to understand Benjamin's personality as that of a pursuer, I saw the body of Christ coming to a place of *pursuing* after God as we've never done before. His response to our seeking after Him will be to pour out His blessings on us. Benjamites must *pursue* God in order to receive their blessing.

> *People from the Negev will occupy the mountains of*
> *Esau, and people from the foothills will possess the land*
> *of the Philistines. They will occupy the fields of Ephraim*
> *and Samaria, and Benjamin will possess Gilead.*
> —Obadiah 1:19

Gilead means "a heap of witnesses; rolling forever." The Word of God says that Benjamin shall possess a mountain of testimonies. Benjamites will have a pile of testimonies of every kind—from overcoming envy, strife, worry, depression, jealousy, lust, gossip, complaining, road rage, and selfish ambition to drug addiction, alcoholism, sexual immorality, and impurity of spirit, soul, and body. We will live to hear Christians testifying without fear of repercussion, "God delivered me from drugs," or, "Alcoholics Anonymous couldn't help me, but God helped me." Christians saying, "I tried to sell my body on the streets, but I found out that the only thing that could truly satisfy my longings was to sell out to God Almighty."

Benjamin sits on a *mountain* of testimonies. The Benjamite church will not be made up of people who were born with silver spoons in their mouths—people who society said would never amount to anything will establish it. And they'll testify without shame and condemnation because they so desire that the world will know the lengths to which God will go to rescue the perishing. The world gave up on them but God didn't!

Benjamin knows how to praise God

The tribe of Benjamin was known to be people of praise in the sanctuary.

> *Your procession has come into view, O God, the procession of my God and King into the sanctuary. In front are the singers, after them the musicians; with them are the maidens playing tambourines. Praise God in the great congregation; praise the Lord in the assembly of Israel. There is the little tribe of Benjamin, leading them....*
>
> —Psalm 68:24-27

There is young Benjamin, walking with God. He isn't behind the singers or the musicians—he's not behind the dancers. He's walking out front. Nobody knows how to praise like Benjamin. Nobody knows how to worship like Benjamin. Benjamin has been through some tough stuff in his life. He knows that at birth his mother called him the child of her sorrow. But he's also heard his father say, "No, I renounce that prophecy. You are the son of my right hand."

THE LAST-DAY BENJAMITE CHURCH IS BEING PREPARED TO GENERATE MORE PROPHETIC AND APOSTOLIC MINISTRIES THAN AT ANY OTHER TIME IN CHURCH HISTORY.

The tribe of Benjamin produced many great prophets and apostles. You need to become familiar with the Benjamites who served God. You need to know about Ehud, Mordecai, Jonathan, Saul, Mephibosheth, Esther, and Paul. Why? The last-day Benjamite church is being prepared to generate more prophetic and apostolic ministries than at any other time in church history. The word *apostle* literally means "one that is sent out." In this last-day church, prophets and apostles are being raised up.

Don't underestimate today's youth—your own children, teens in your kids' school or church youth group—even the worst of them! You and I absolutely must stop exhibiting the attitude that we've never been as bad as they are…as though we never had a rebellious thought in our lives. Come on! Get real…with yourself. But look at you now. You may think that teenager in your life will never amount to anything, but you are so wrong!

I've yet to meet a teenager in the youth group at my church who is worse than I was at his or her age. Don't tell me what God can't do with these kids. They will be our apostles and prophets. They may not worship God the way we do…they may not dress like we dress, act like we act, or talk like we talk. *So what?*

They may look like a generation that doesn't even know how to pull their pants up…they may be mooning the whole world. And that's about the attitude they have. But I'm getting ready to shock you—they have a *right* to feel that way! Why? Because this world has not given them a good example to follow.

But God has blessed them and called them to fulfill His eternal plan and purpose for mankind in these last days. Others may call them incorrigible—He calls them a chosen generation.

Not only has He called them, but He has equipped them with everything they will ever need to do battle with the devil…and win. When they come into the Kingdom, they will have a five-fold blessing—resources unlimited. No wonder they will say, *I can do all things through Christ which strengtheneth me* (Philippians 4:13 KJV).

Do you understand why I am so excited…so passionate about what God is going to do in these last days? I sought the Lord for a wonderful, new approach and presentation of the gospel in this last hour that would reach trans-generational groups. I earnestly pursued Him, because the cry of my heart is to minister in a way that will keep on satisfying the old while reaching the young.

25

God let me know that I needed to become a true Benjamite—a radically desperate pursuer of Him—exhibiting love for Him with reckless abandon and an insatiable appetite to help gather in the last-day harvest. He said if I would do that, He would bring in Benjamite children by the multitudes. He showed me that the answer is simple—keep the praise high, the worship deep, the affection flowing, the spirit of Benjamin pursuing. From that, God will develop a generation that is fit to usher in the second coming of Christ.

Adapting a five-fold, destiny-changing plan to *your* life

As a Benjamite, *you are called, anointed, and set aside* to be God's man or woman in this last day. You are a child of God's right hand. Actually, coming to this realization is the first part of the five-fold plan that will change your destiny. The Benjamin spirit pursues God, but to do that, the spirit of compromise absolutely must be obliterated in your life. It has to go—no ifs, ands, or buts. You must make a decision that, no matter what happens, you're going with God and His ways all the way.

1. YOU ARE CALLED, ANOINTED, AND SET ASIDE.

2. YOU ARE EQUIPPED.

3. YOU HAVE THE POWER TO CHANGE.

4. YOU HAVE BEEN GIVEN AUTHORITY.

5. YOU HAVE ALL THAT YOU NEED TIMES FIVE.

Benjamin received *five times* the blessing of any of the other brothers seated at Joseph's table. That is your inheritance—your birthright as a Benjamite! *You are equipped to be all that God has called you to be.* Notice that I said, "You *are* equipped," and not that "you *will be* equipped." You are equipped as a blood-bought, Holy Ghost-filled, sanctified child of the living God. This knowledge is the second key to the five-fold discovery process.

While evil men and impostors will go from bad to worse, deceiving and being deceived…as for you, contin-

ue in what you have learned and have become convinced of.... All Scripture is God-breathed and is useful for teaching, rebuking, correcting and training in righteousness, so that the man of God may be thoroughly equipped for every good work.

—2 Timothy 3:13,14,16,17

Number three. *You have the power to change* from what you have been to what God wants you to be. It is a fact—believe it! Believe it about yourself starting right now.

And he [Jesus] *said: "I tell you the truth, unless you change and become like little children, you will never enter the kingdom of heaven. Therefore, whoever humbles himself like this child is the greatest in the kingdom of heaven. And whoever welcomes a little child like this in my name welcomes me. But if anyone causes one of these little ones who believe in me to sin, it would be better for him to have a large millstone hung around his neck and to be drowned in the depths of the sea.*

—Matthew 18:3-6

You have the power to change. There are no limits on you except those that you impose upon yourself. No doubt about it, you will be bombarded with self-doubt and fear. You'll want to quit trying—perhaps every day. Cooperate with God and don't give up. Time is a great healer. It is amazing what time and distance from old, destructive thought and action patterns can do for you. Benjamites have Holy Ghost power! Take hold of it! Who knows that God hasn't brought you to this place in history for such a time as this? Choose to change!

For the grace of God...teaches us to say "No" to ungodliness and worldly passions, and to live self-controlled, upright and godly lives in this present age, while we wait for the blessed hope—the glorious appearing of our great God and Savior, Jesus Christ, who gave himself for us to redeem us from all wickedness and to purify for himself a people that are his very own, eager to do what is good. These, then, are the things you should teach. Encourage and rebuke with all authority....

—Titus 2:11-15

God has given you the authority to be and do whatever you need to be and do in every situation, functioning in all the gifts of the Spirit—part four of the plan to change your destiny. You have the ability to overcome all obstacles that are in your way. I love to quote a great lady, Kay Cole James, who repeatedly demonstrates that gracefully walking in God-given authority can take you places you never dreamed of going.

Mrs. James is director of the Office of Personnel Management in the Bush administration and is in charge of 1.8 million members of the federal workforce. She also served in the administrations of former presidents Reagan and Bush. She says, "I was born on a kitchen table to a poor black woman on welfare who had four children already and an alcoholic husband. Today my mother would be advised that the "most compassionate" thing to do would be to abort me! I spent my early years in a public housing project...a half-mile from the field where the Ku Klux Klan held cross-burnings."

Mrs. James calls herself "a survivor, an overcomer of this obstacle course called America." Eventually God placed her in the corridors of power at the White House. She realized that God had given her the power and authority to do whatever she needed to do and be what she needed to be in every situation in which she found herself.

28

In her book, *Never Forget,* Mrs. James writes, "If we as individuals and a nation don't embrace this same overcomer identity, we will waste precious time and energy in vain pity. Just as God used Esther to save her people by placing her in a strategic position at a critical time, we must focus on what we can do, not on what's being done to us."

The fifth part of the five-fold plan to change your destiny is to make up your mind that *God has provided everything you need times five* to make a difference in your world. That's a powerful statement, and it is absolutely true. As a God-ordained overcomer, you have five times more resources to draw upon than any power or obstacle you will ever encounter. And because the greatest battles we fight are within our own minds, you have five times the ability to face down discouragement, doubt, and unbelief, without engaging your mood-swinging emotions.

Bestselling author, conference speaker, and television host, Joyce Meyer, writes in one of my all-time favorite books, *Battlefield of the Mind,* "God places dreams and visions in the hearts of His people; they begin as little "seeds." Just as a woman has a seed planted into her womb

> "THE ENEMY DOESN'T WANT YOU AND ME TO GET OUR MIND IN AGREEMENT WITH OUR SPIRIT."
> —JOYCE MEYER

when she becomes pregnant, so we become "pregnant," so to speak, with the things God speaks and promises. During the "pregnancy," Satan works hard to try and get us to "abort" our dreams. One of the tools he uses is doubt; another is unbelief. Both of these work against the mind.

"Faith is a product of the spirit; it is a spiritual force. The enemy doesn't want you and me to get our mind in agreement with our spirit. He knows that if God places faith in us to do a thing, and we get positive and start consistently believing that we can actually do it, then we will do considerable damage to his kingdom.

"The devil brings storms into your life to intimidate you. During a storm, remember that the mind is the battlefield. Don't make your decisions based on your thoughts or feelings, but check with your spirit. When you do, you will find the same vision that was there in the beginning."

For as he thinks in his heart, so is he...(Proverbs 23:7 AMP). Now you're five-for-five in God's plan to change your destiny. When you align your thoughts and actions with God's thoughts about you, you will realize and act upon the fact that God is your Father and you are His child. You were raised by your Father, and you have made a quality decision to walk with Him daily. You can do exploits, Benjamite, until you win!

Repeat the Benjamites' Daily Prayer with me:

> *Father, let my life be*
> *Your glorious contradiction*
> *to the world's definition of normal.*

3

Traits of a Benjamite

*These were the men who came to David at Ziklag,
while he was banished from the presence of Saul son of
Kish (they were among the warriors who helped him in
battle; they were armed with bows and were able to shoot
arrows or to sling stones right-handed or left-handed;
they were kinsmen of Saul from the tribe of Benjamin).*
—1 Chronicles 12:1,2

*At once the Benjamites mobilized twenty-six thou-
sand swordsmen from their towns, in addition to seven
hundred chosen men from those living in Gibeah. Among
all these soldiers there were seven hundred chosen men
who were left-handed, each of whom could sling a stone
at a hair and not miss.*
—Judges 20:15,16

The fact that Benjamites were left-handed is first referred to
in Judges 3:15 to describe a bold, left-handed avenger named Ehud,
a member of the tribe of Benjamin. We're going to talk about him at
length in this chapter.

Just the fact that the Benjamites' left-handedness is mentioned
in the Bible testifies to the fact that it was a somewhat unique trait
that appeared to be hereditary. Moreover, this particular tribe had
become known for its left-handed fighters. They were actually
ambidextrous, "capable of using both hands with equal facility."
This unique skill certainly could come in handy in times of war.
What rare, exceptional, distinctive, and uncommon characteristics
has God gifted you with, Benjamite?

Benjamites have character

Can you imagine going out shopping for a book entitled, *The Book of Failures?* Probably not. Yet many theologians refer to the Old Testament book of Judges as "the book of failures"—but further investigation reveals that Judges examines the lives of some real champions of character. We will employ one such guide to lead us on a journey of hope and deliverance.

Please keep in mind that the record shows that left-handed Benjamites will *always* produce a deliverer.

Once again the Israelites did evil in the eyes of the Lord, and because they did this evil the Lord gave Eglon king of Moab power over Israel. Getting the Ammonites and Amalekites to join him, Eglon came and attacked Israel, and they took possession of the City of Palms. The Israelites were subject to Eglon king of Moab for eighteen years. Again the Israelites cried out to the Lord, and he gave them a deliverer—Ehud, a left-handed man, the son of Gera the Benjamite. The Israelites sent him with tribute to Eglon king of Moab. Now Ehud had made a double-edged sword about a foot and a half long, which he strapped to his right thigh under his clothing. He presented the tribute to Eglon king of Moab, who was a very fat man. After Ehud had presented the tribute, he sent on their way the men who had carried it. At the idols near Gilgal he himself turned back and said, "I have a secret message for you, O king."

The king said, "Quiet!" And all his attendants left him. Ehud then approached him while he was sitting alone in the upper room of his summer palace and said, "I have a message from God for you." As the king rose from his seat, Ehud reached with his left hand, drew the sword from his right thigh and plunged it into the king's belly. Even the handle sank in after the blade, which came out his back. Ehud did not pull the sword out, and the fat closed in over it. Then Ehud went out to the porch; he shut the doors of the upper room behind him and locked them. After he had gone, the servants came and found the doors of the upper room locked. They said, "He must be relieving himself in the inner room of the house." They waited to the point of embarrassment, but when he did not open the doors of the room, they took a key and unlocked them. There they saw their lord fallen to the floor, dead.

While they waited, Ehud got away. He passed by the idols and escaped to Seirah. When he arrived there, he blew a trumpet in the hill country of Ephraim, and the Israelites went down with him from the hills, with him leading them. "Follow me," he ordered, "for the Lord has given Moab, your enemy, into your hands." So they followed him down and, taking possession of the fords of the Jordan that led to Moab, they allowed no one to cross over. At that time they struck down about ten thousand Moabites, all vigorous and strong; not a man escaped. That day Moab was made subject to Israel, and the land had peace for eighty years.

—Judges 3:12-30

These are very descriptive verses—nothing is hidden here. Considering the times (historians chart the timeline of Israel's twelve judges as roughly 1,220 to 1,050 BC), this grotesque and even crude narration sounds remarkably similar to the times in which we live today. Let's consider the impact of this violent encounter between Eglon and Ehud.

Eglon is the energetic king of the Moabites, a proud people who were always set against the people of God. Do you know anyone who might be aptly described as "always being set against" the people or things of God? The Moabites seized Jericho during a period of decline among the Israelites after the death of Othniel. Notice in verse 13, he took "...the City of Palms...." This literally means that he drove out Jericho's previous tenants and took possession of everything they owned —he confiscated their *stuff.*

> SATAN DOES NOT WANT US TO POSSESS WHAT IS RIGHTFULLY OURS...BUT I'M TIRED OF THE DEVIL STEALING MY STUFF!

When I saw that, the Lord reminded me that Satan, the enemy of our soul, does NOT want us to possess what is rightfully ours—what Christ died and was resurrected to provide for us. I don't know about you, but I'm tired of the devil stealing my stuff. And I'm not just referring to material things. I'm talking about the devil's efforts to steal my victory, my joy, and my peace of mind, my health, the success and well-being of my family—important things that have nothing whatsoever to do with material accumulation.

I'm tired of it! In fact, I've had all I'm going to take from him. I've determined that he is not going to intimidate me out of what my Savior sacrificed His life to possess for me. What God has made available to me is mine. And no big, fat man is going to come along and tell me what to do with it or take it away from me!

It's a decision—a choice—and I'm making it here and now. No more! I'm holding on to every single one of God's blessings for me. Any opportunity I've given Satan to mess with what's mine is finished as of now! How about you? Are you ready to close the door to the devil's plan for your life?

To whom or to what are you paying tribute?

Eglon demanded that the people pay him taxes annually. I picture this big, fat, proud king, sitting on his big, wide, oversized throne, forcing his subjects to finance his excessive lifestyle. This scenario immediately brings to mind the enormous number of saints in the body of Christ who are addicted or "pay tribute" to certain habits that are excessive and completely unlike God. Every time the opportunity presents itself, they submit to these harmful and destructive habits—excessive eating, drinking, spending, talking, and accumulating, or worry, depression, bitterness, unforgiveness, and strife…to name only a few. To whom or to what are you paying tribute?

We have to stop submitting to the big, fat "kings" in our lives and stand up and say, "No, sir, you deserve no respect from me, and you'll receive no further tribute. I'm not going to be 'taxed' (vexed, worried, driven, strained, encumbered) by you. You will be a burden to me no longer!"

I'm talking about getting your *stuff* back. It's time for you to have a face-off with the devil and say, "You're not going to intimidate me anymore. I've found out who I am in Christ Jesus. Everything that God says is mine is mine. Don't you even try to come close to it. I don't care where you're from, what your name is, how big you are, or what you have to say. This is my stuff, and you can't take it from me. I'm a Benjamite!"

Benjamites are winners!

Have you ever noticed how the enemy uses people to help him maintain control over you? Eglon used the Ammonites and Amalekites as his enforcers. The Ammonites went along with whatever any authority figure wanted to do—they were just people pleasers. They didn't want Eglon coming after them, so if he gave them an order to go over to Jericho and stir up some trouble, they went.

The Ammonite spirit of compromise is loose today in those who come alongside you and say, "It's okay. It's just a little sin. Who's going to know? I'm with you all the way, pal. Go ahead and do it—I'll never tell anybody, and besides, you deserve it." Do you know any people-pleasing compromisers? They're a huge part of today's church.

The Amalekites, on the other hand, were a nomadic, marauding people who were avowed enemies of Israel. They were never strong enough to have their own army, so they worked as mercenaries, huddling in little groups until someone hired them to be a raiding party. We know them today as gossipers, complainers, whiners, and backbiters. Relationships with them are what some psychologists refer to as *toxic* (harmful, destructive, even poisonous) associations. They're not strong enough to act for themselves, but if someone else is causing trouble, they want to be a part of it. The church is full of them.

If you currently mingle with some Amalekite spirits, you need to disengage yourself from them—it isn't healthy for you to hang around…not even if you're trying to help them. It will hinder your progress. Not everyone is willing to do what it takes to attain the Benjamin blessing. Not everyone is going to go where you are going. Evaluate all of your relationships. Are any of them blocking your vision? Remember, you become what you allow yourself to hang around. Cut them off, Benjamin.

For eighteen long years, Israel had been bullied by the oppressive rule of King Eglon. Amazingly, his name literally means "a bull calf." You may remember a bully from your early school days. He never really did anything himself. He had others do things for him, making him appear to be tough. *Bully* is just another name for intimidation, which is based solely on appearance. It's time for the saints to take a closer look at the Eglons in their lives and say, "You're not going to bully me anymore. I've come to take you out in Jesus' name."

Let's go after the bully spirit of intimidation—the BIG devil. Always remember this: You can resist the devil. How? First, you have to acknowledge that he actually exists. Next, realize the truth of 2 Corinthians 2:11, ...*For we are not unaware of his* [Satan's] *schemes,* including temptation, slander, and false accusations. Finally, make a quality decision to firmly oppose his attacks in the name of Jesus Christ.

You and I have spiritual authority over the adversary, according to 1 John 4:4, ...*the one who is in you is greater than the one who is in the world.* That's just one of the benefits Jesus purchased for you with His life, death, and resurrection!

In order to deal with the big issues in our lives, look with me at Judges 3:15, *Again the Israelites cried out to the Lord....* The word *cry* here literally means, "to shriek from anguish or danger." In other words, when the people had had enough and began to cry out to God for help, He sent them a deliverer.

During my childhood, when my mama said, "I've had just about enough of this," everybody ducked for cover. Those seven little words sent a message to each of her children that she'd been pushed as far as she was willing to go. She was about to take care of business, and nothing would ever be the same. Have you had enough? You must awaken the Benjamin spirit of deliverance in your life.

WE'RE HERE AT THIS PRECISE MOMENT IN HISTORY BECAUSE GOD SPECIFICALLY DESIGNED US TO DELIVER *THIS* GENERATION.

When you come to your senses and decide you've had all you're going to take from Satan, things will begin to change. God will raise up a deliverer. The same goes for the church. Today I believe an entire generation of Benjamites who have been here all the time are now stepping up to the plate. I believe God has kept us for this hour and this generation. He is raising us up so we can take care of some serious business before He returns.

You and I have a personal responsibility to our generation. We weren't called to yesterday's generation, and we're not called to tomorrow's generation. We're here at this precise moment in history because God specifically designed us to deliver *this* generation.

Benjamites become what they're looking for

Benjamites can handle any challenge this generation can devise. It belongs to us, but we must identify ourselves, willingly stand up, and say, "Enough is enough. We are the deliverers—the rescuers. We know the way. We can lead you out of your personal darkness—your bondage to addictions of the flesh. We can introduce you to the Savior of your soul who will heal your sick body and bless you so you can become a blessing to others. We're left-handed Benjamites, and we're bad to the bone." The only thing standing between your victory and you is you—you're going to recoup everything you've lost. You are not too late, too young, or too old!

How do we prepare ourselves for confrontation? We have to start by building up confidence in God and reinforcing our self-esteem because the devil is committed to our total annihilation. Maybe you've been whipped around by the devil so much that you're starting to believe that he can whip you. Well, he can't unless you let him.

You must decide that you don't have to give in to ungodly habits. You don't have to expose yourself to the weaknesses of your flesh. You don't have to stay the way you are. God didn't make you to just "be." You're a Benjamite! ...*In all things we* [you and I] *are more than conquerors through him who loved us* (Romans 8:37)!

Benjamin refuses to compromise

Notice this man, Ehud. His name means "undivided." *A double minded man is unstable in all his ways* (James 1:8 KJV). Benjamites are stable—the Benjamin generation is full of people with undivided loyalties. They don't have a double heart or a heart within a heart. No, Benjamites are committed. They're willing to go through the valley with you. They'll weather your storm as if it were their own. They have a union with you and with God.

Benjamites aren't fickle people who want to be on your team as long as everything is going well, but disappear when the going gets rough. Ehud was a bold, left-handed Benjamite who was tired of Eglon's oppression—so he took matters into his own hands. He organized a party of steel-nerved men who pretended to bring tribute to the fat dictator. He didn't look for deliverance—he *was* deliverance personified.

At this time, the tribe of Benjamin had been reduced from an army of 40,000 to approximately 700 fighting men. God has a way of trimming away all the excess so He can get down to the real thing. When Ehud shoved that eighteen-inch dagger—one inch for every year of Israel's oppression—into Eglon's fat belly, the point came out of his back and the handle was swallowed up in the fat.

Are you ready to take back what's been taken from you and your family? It's time for you to begin enjoying the fruits of the Spirit, *...love, joy, peace, patience, kindness, goodness, faithfulness, gentleness, and self-control. Against such things there is no law* (see Galatians 5:22,23).

BENJAMITES... THOSE WHO COME TO PROMINENCE IN THE END-TIME—ARE DEADLY ACCURATE IN THEIR WARFARE.

The Benjamites I'm talking about—those who come to prominence in the end-time—are deadly accurate in their warfare. We know exactly who and where the enemy is, and we don't miss! To miss the mark is to sin, and sin doesn't dominate us—including the sin of compromise. Some people wake up missing the mark and go to bed missing the mark. But as a Benjamite, you were not born into sin, to miss the mark. Hide God's Word in your heart, Benjamin, and sing with the psalmist, *I have hidden your word in my heart that I might not sin against you* (Psalm 119:11).

Left-handed literally means "shut out of the right." Benjamite, you may be left-handed, but you're not left out. As we saw in the biblical account, for the Benjamites, being left-handed literally meant "to be ambidextrous." The most dangerous batter on a baseball team is a switch hitter because he can swing with equal power and skill from either side.

The same is true in the sport of basketball. The rule is, "If you can't go left, you ain't got game." If you want to play in the NBA, you'd better be able to go left. My son started playing basketball at a very young age. I would make Dustin take the ball and hold his right hand to his side, never touching the ball with his right hand. At first he was so miserable. He'd be dribbling and go for the ball with his right hand. I'd tell him, "Don't you touch it." When you go into a basketball game, the person guarding you is going to guard you to your right because most people are right-handed. He's going to make you go to your left just to see if you can. If he sees that you can, he's going to think 'Uh-oh, he's got game!'"

> *ALWAYS CHALLENGE YOUR WEAKNESS INSTEAD OF TRYING TO CONCEAL IT.*

The body of Christ has got to have "game." Ambidextrous, right or left. When the devil tries to cut us off on the right, we must have the ability to switch and go left.

I'll tell you a secret about playing basketball that applies to life as a Christian—*always challenge your weakness* instead of trying to conceal it. If you can't go left, then learn to go left. If you know you can't go left very well, at least come into the game dribbling the ball left-handed. If you come in right-handed, the opposition knows he can challenge you to the left. But when you get the ball and go left immediately, it makes the other guy think. If you want to improve your game, you must play with better players.

Challenge your weakness. Go after your weakness and say, "Where I'm weak is where I'm going to win today." In other words, set out to prove that what used to defeat you is not going to defeat you anymore. Challenge it until you can do it. You can go left. Never allow yourself to get caught off guard. When the devil gets on you, go around him. If you can't go around him, go over him. If you can't go over him, go through him. But get to the basket and score! It doesn't matter what life throws at you, you *can* hit it. Benjamites are ambidextrous!

Back to Ehud. Although he lived in a captive, subservient nation, he was an improviser. The Bible says Ehud made a dagger that was eighteen inches long. The Israelites had been in captivity for eighteen years. Imagine Ehud working on his dagger, saying under his breath, "For every year you oppressed me, Eglon, I'm making an inch of knife blade for you. As a matter of fact, I'm going to lose the entire blade in you, handle and all. When I bury it in your belly, I'm not interested in finding it anymore. I've got one shot at you, so I have to take you out the first time!"

> BENJAMITES REFUSE TO LIVE IN THE SOULISH REALM, ALLOWING THEMSELVES TO BE CONTROLLED BY THEIR MIND (THOUGHTS), WILL, AND EMOTIONS.

You say the devil's been after you for ten years? Well, you've got ten good scriptures to shove down his throat. When the devil opens his mouth, hit him. When he gives you one problem, give him one scripture. If he gives you seven kinds of trouble, give God seven kinds of praise. The Benjamin Church needs to rise up in the last hour with a powerful left hand that says we are going to end the oppression in our lives. Don't wait to start praising until you *feel* like it. Benjamites refuse to live in the *soulish* realm, allowing themselves to be controlled by their mind (thoughts), will, and emotions.

I believe the last-day church will be a master of improvising. *To improvise* means, "to make do with whatever you have." Use what you have. Do you have a voice? No one said you have to sing on the praise team to give the devil fits. The Bible doesn't say sing a pretty song—it says *make a joyful noise...* (Psalm 66:1). I've been praying for God to baptize the body of Christ with a Benjamin spirit.

As you read the book of Judges, you'll find some unorthodox weapons and strategy. There are not many traditional tactics to be found. But *every* weapon, every improvised battle, brought victory. Shamgar, the farmer, used an ox goad. The Philistines had closed off the highway, so he had to walk the long way home every day. One day he said, "I've had enough! I'm not going home the long way today—I'm taking the good road." He got his farming tool and went looking for the Philistines. He had to bust a few heads with his ox goad, but he opened up the road and went on his way. (See Judges 3.)

Why is the road rough? Because we *allow* the enemy to make it rough. You've got to get so sick of the rough road that you say, "That's it. I'm not taking that rough road any more. I'm taking the highway." *As iron sharpens iron, so one man sharpens another* (Proverbs 27:17). What does it mean to *sharpen* another person? Just as rubbing the smooth blade against a stone or a rough piece of iron or steel sharpens knives, people sharpen one another by expressing opinions, exchanging ideas and information, and sharing different perspectives.

Shamgar took the sharp stick he'd been poking cows with and poked some Philistines with it. He knew how to use his ox goad—he was familiar with it. He didn't need a new weapon to win that old war. People always want to try out something new and they end up with something strange. But you don't need a new weapon. What God has already put in your hands will work very well.

For Jael, it was a tent peg. For Gideon, it was a torch and a lamp. For Samson, it was a jawbone. God let a donkey die in that spot long ago because He knew Samson would need his jawbone.

Stop looking for a sword when God's given you a jawbone. Quit looking for something new when God's already given you what you need. You're still looking for "a new word" when you haven't used the old word. You're looking for the Hebrew definition when you don't even know the English definition. Use what you've got. Be innovative. What do you have in your hand?

> QUIT LOOKING FOR SOMETHING NEW WHEN GOD'S ALREADY GIVEN YOU WHAT YOU NEED.

Ehud took Eglon a present. Are you ready to take the enemy a present? We've got a present for the devil. It's a message from God—"You are defeated!" Let the devil know that you're serious. This isn't something you heard from just anybody. God said it. Ehud went to see Eglon with a message from God.

What was the secret strength of the shepherd boy, David? It wasn't in his slingshot or five smooth stones, but his amazing trust and faith in God and a divinely inspired message for any enemy of God—in this case, the nine-feet-tall giant, Goliath. He said, "You come against me with all your stuff, but I come against you in the name of the Lord of hosts, whom I serve and whom you have defied. Therefore, tall guy, today you die!"

How do you get a message from God? You listen to Him. I am coming to you today with a message from God that says if you want the oppression of your life and spirit to be over, it's over today. You decide.

Ehud was innovative, an improviser, and idols made him mad. He was on his way home with his guys. They'd delivered the present…they had paid tribute. Ehud was walking out. When he got to Gilgal, he saw all the idols set up to represent Eglon, the oppressive king. Ehud became incensed and told his guys to go ahead. There was something he needed to take care of, so he went back to Eglon's palace.

"Sir, can we have a talk? I have a message from God for you."

"Of course," Eglon replied, "What is it?"

So Ehud walked back in past the king's attendants, with the dagger on his right side. He was able to slip in by being innovative…sneaky even. Most soldiers carried their swords on their left sides because they were right-handed. Ehud walked in with his dagger hidden on his right side. When he approached the king, he pulled it out with his left hand and plunged it into the king.

The final thing to notice about Ehud is that he was an individual leader who also was interdependent upon other relationships. He wasn't an island unto himself. So many Christians and leaders today become isolated. Rather than cultivating strong affiliations, they do their own thing. There are too many loners in the body of Christ and not enough individuals who will dare to be leaders.

Ehud blew a trumpet to summon the men of Israel down from the hills. When they had assembled, he said, "Follow me." Under his leadership, the Israelites killed some ten thousand men of Moab and brought deliverance and freedom to their nation. The Bible says there was peace in the land for eighty years after that.

The Benjamin Church is a gathering of leaders. The apostle Paul, who was a Benjamite, said, "Follow me as I follow Christ." Christ is looking for husbands who will lead their families. A Benjamite wife whose husband wants to stay home says she's taking the kids and going to church. Leaders are willing to step out and take responsibility.

Hosea saw in chapter 5, verse 8 of his prophecy that Benjamin was a leader. He said, "Blow your trumpet in Gibeah, blow it in

Ramah, and blow it in Beth-aven, but Benjamin shall lead on." Benjamites will always be leading.

A leader is someone who inspires confidence so that others want to follow. If you think you are beaten, you are. If you think you dare not, you don't. If you think you can't win, it's almost certain you won't. Life's battles don't always go to the stronger or faster man, but sooner or later the man who wins is the man who thinks he can. A true leader says, "I will find a way to win. If I can do it right-handed, I will. If I need to work from the left side, I can do that. I'll do what I have to do because I refuse to be beaten. I am never down. I am either up or I'm getting up."

If you're a Benjamite, you always ought to be looking for a way to defeat and win the victory...and lead those around you to accomplish more than they ever thought possible. You are resourceful and innovative. You can change tactics to turn the course of any battle.

As a last-day Benjamite, you are a son of God's right hand, but you can be left-handed if necessary! Lead on, Benjamin!

4

The Benjamite Mission

Benjamites are leaders. You were born to be a leader. You are called to be a leader. You are a leader.

This generation of Christians is feeling a sense of urgency and expectancy to locate its purpose and activate a long-awaited transition. We are poised for a changing of the guard, when a new group of leaders comes to the forefront of God's army. These will be the players in the final episode of God's eternal plan.

We've examined the story of Ehud, who had no problem in his day assuming his role in leadership. Let's go now to 1 Samuel 14 to evaluate another important scenario of transition and consider the heart of a young Benjamite named Jonathan.

> One day Jonathan son of Saul said to the young man bearing his armor, "Come, let's go over to the Philistine outpost on the other side." But he did not tell his father.
> On each side of the pass that Jonathan intended to cross to reach the Philistine outpost was a cliff; one was called Bozez, the other Seneh. One cliff stood to the north toward Micmash, the other to the south toward Geba. Jonathan said to his young armor-bearer, "Come, let's go over to the outpost of those uncircumcised fellows. Perhaps the Lord will act in our behalf. Nothing can hinder the Lord from saving, whether by many or by few."
> "Do all that you have in mind," his armor-bearer said. "Go ahead; I am with you heart and soul."
> Jonathan said, "Come then; we will cross over toward the men and let them see us. If they say to us,

'Wait there until we come to you,' we will stay where we are and not go up to them. But if they say, 'Come up to us,' we will climb up, because that will be our sign that the Lord has given them into our hands."

So both of them showed themselves to the Philistine outpost. "Look!" said the Philistines. "The Hebrews are crawling out of the holes they were hiding in." The men of the outpost shouted to Jonathan and his armor-bearer, "Come up to us and we will teach you a lesson." So Jonathan said to his armor-bearer, "Climb up after me; the Lord has given them into the hand of Israel."

Jonathan climbed up, using his hands and feet, with his armor-bearer right behind him. The Philistines fell before Jonathan, and his armor-bearer followed and killed behind him. In that first attack Jonathan and his armor-bearer killed some twenty men in an area of about half an acre.

—1 Samuel 14:1,4-14

Benjamites are leaders

Ravenous wolves can't be still. Jacob had described his son Benjamin, "He is a ravenous wolf" (see Genesis 49:27). Wolves are always hungry, adventurous, looking around, licking their chops...and with a wild look in their eyes that says, "I am getting ready to do something radical."

Jonathan looked at his armor-bearer and said, "Let's you and I just go up and attack that whole army of uncircumcised Philistines!" And his armor-bearer was crazy too. He said, "Let's go! Lead on, I'm with you heart and soul." Here are two brave, brash, and obviously bored young men. It's not in their nature to be still. Israel had been at an impasse for six years, intimidated and controlled by the warlike, domineering Philistines. One day Jonathan had just had enough and decided he wasn't going to take it any more.

He stood up, shook himself, and announced that he was ready to launch a mission. He was ready to fulfill his duty. "Let's go," he said. "Maybe the Lord will help us. And if He does, it doesn't matter if we have lots of fighters or just a few. With God on our side, nothing can keep us from winning!"

Throughout both the Old and New Testaments, when the people of God got into trying predicaments, there was always a Benjamite that arose out of the heap of ruin to lead Israel to a triumphant victory. Hosea 5:8 says, *"Sound the trumpet in Gibeah, the horn in Ramah. Raise the battle cry in Beth Aven; lead on, O Benjamin."*

When Benjamites get going, God gets going. God loves to move where Benjamites are. If you don't believe that, ask the apostles Paul and Silas. Paul was from the tribe of Benjamin, and while he and Silas were in a jail cell with their feet fastened in stocks, they started praying and singing (see Acts 16:25). God must have said, "I've got to get going in that jailhouse, because there is a Benjamite down there crying out for My attention."

In short, if you want God to move, you've got to move. And if you're the leader of a mission, you've got to be out in front.

Psalm 68:24-27 describes ...*the procession of my God and King into the sanctuary. In front are the singers, after them the musicians; with them are the maidens playing tambourines. Praise God in the great congregation; praise the Lord in the assembly of Israel. There is the little tribe of Benjamin, leading them....*

When Jonathan set out on his mission, he had to prove he was a leader. He found one guy who would follow him even in the face of absolutely incredible odds. "You lead the way," said the armor-bearer, "I'll be with you all the way."

The passage of leadership

The Bible says there were cliffs on both sides of the pass

Jonathan intended to cross to reach the Philistine outpost. The one to the north toward Micmash was called Bozez, and the one to the south toward Geba was called Senah.

PURITY AND PERSEVERANCE PRODUCE INTEGRITY—NO COMPROMISE.

Being a leader is never just a walk in the park. There are certain *cliffs* we must climb to become effective. One cliff represents purity and another represents perseverance. Purity and perseverance produce integrity—no compromise.

People are not going to follow a person who lacks integrity for any length of time. And people are reluctant to follow those who haven't been through anything. *Integrity* means "to be whole; complete; sound; firm adherence to a code or standard of values."

God is raising up a generation of leaders who believe in holiness, integrity, and character, and they've been through some stern tests to prove it. So when you feel that you've never been through so much hell in all your life, just realize that you have a choice. You can respond in one of two ways—you can let it consume and destroy you or you can let it make you stronger.

Tests and trials are not sent to kill you—God allows them to build you, prove you, and make you stronger. In other words, you don't get strength for the battle—you get strength from the battle. God must believe in your purity, your perseverance, and your ability to go through or you wouldn't be facing so much trouble. ***The passage to leadership is integrity.***

The power of leadership

Leadership is not measured in numbers—it is measured in *influence,* which is "the power to indirectly or intangibly affect a person or event." Some form of influence affects everyone. Benjamites are always looking around—observing the strengths and gifts in potential allies and friends. We seek to increase our circle of influence.

Jesus led by influence, which was enacted by two words, "Follow me." When Ehud faced and ultimately killed Eglon, he came back to the Israelites and influenced them to take action with two words, "Follow me." In the Old Testament account of Jonathan's mission, he said exactly the same two words to his faithful armor-bearer: "Follow me."

I'm told that Israeli military leaders have the highest casualty rate of any army because they never *send* their troops to do battle without *leading* the charge themselves. They position themselves before a column of troops and say, "Charge!" They *lead* the charge—they don't just stand back while troops under their command risk life and limb to enter the fray. Leaders don't say, "Go get 'em," but "Follow me." In other words, "I'm willing to go ahead and take the first blow. Who will go with me?" As the famous Benjamite, Paul, said, *Be ye followers of me, even as I also am of Christ* (1 Corinthians 11:1 KJV).

> LEADERSHIP IS NOT MEASURED IN NUMBERS—IT IS MEASURED IN INFLUENCE.

It's impossible to follow someone who isn't going anywhere. Children can't follow the example of a father who is never home, who never has time for them. Wives cannot follow husbands they can't respect—husbands who aren't going anywhere themselves. When a person who would be a leader says, "Follow me," he'd better be moving! *The power of leadership is the influence of personal example!*

The position of leadership

In the account of his bold mission, *Jonathan said, "Come, then; we will cross over toward the men and let them see us"* (1 Samuel 14:8). True leaders are willing to step out in times of adversity. False leaders hide. When the going gets tough, the tough get going...and others will follow. When conflict arose between the

TRUE LEADERS ARE WILLING TO STEP OUT IN TIMES OF ADVERSITY. FALSE LEADERS HIDE.

Israelites and Philistines at another time, a little shepherd boy named David did not hide among the sheep. Visiting the battlefield, he heard the voice of Goliath and said, "This is my opportunity to oppose this enemy of God." He said, "I'm going out front." His leadership mission brought him face to face with Goliath. *The position of leadership is in front.*

Preparation for leadership

Before Jonathan and his lone follower went out to face the Philistines, they prepared a battle plan. *"If they say to us, 'Wait there until we come to you,' we will stay where we are and not go up to them,"* said Jonathan. *"But if they say, 'Come up to us,' we will climb up, because that will be our sign that the Lord has given them into our hands"* (1 Samuel 14:9,10). Not only were Jonathan and his armor-bearer *positioned* for leadership, but they were also prepared. They had studied the situation, evaluated their options, and made a plan of action. They had made up their minds, and the power of decision made them bold and confident.

Are you ready to rumble? If you want to be a leader, then you'd better do your homework. Pray, seeking the Lord's wisdom. And renew your mind with the Word of God. *Do not conform any longer to the pattern of this world, but be transformed by the renewing of your mind* (Romans 12:2). You can actually be *transformed* if you'll renew your mind in the Word. Again, the decision is yours.

Second Corinthians 3:18 reiterates this important truth, *And we, who with unveiled faces all reflect the Lord's glory, are being transformed into his likeness with ever-increasing glory, which comes from the Lord, who is the Spirit.* Take time to become intimately acquainted with God through His Word. Meditate on the truths you find there and let it change you from the inside out.

Become knowledgeable on all fronts so you can make informed decisions. Close all the gaps that would leave you vulnerable to attack. *Search me, O God, and know my heart; test me and know my anxious thoughts. See if there is any offensive way in me, and lead me in the way everlasting* (Psalm 139:23,24). How does God search us? He examines our hearts and motives. He looks at our personalities and fantasies, observing our *innermost*

> "WHAT HAPPENS *IN* YOU IS MORE IMPORTANT THAN WHAT HAPPENS *TO* YOU."
> —BILL WILSON

thoughts. As Metro Ministries Founder and President Bill Wilson always says, "What happens *in* you is more important than what happens *to* you." Only then are you really ready for a fight. ***True leadership requires preparation.***

The purpose of leadership

The purpose of all leadership is to carry out a mission. Jonathan genuinely believed that he should make no small plans. "It may be that God will give all the enemy into our hands," he said. How convincing was he? How much influence did he wield? "Let's go," said his armor-bearer. "I'm with you all the way." *So both of them showed themselves to the Philistine outpost. "Look!" said the Philistines. "The Hebrews are crawling out of the holes they were hiding in"* (v.11).

The hour has come for the last-day church to embark on its mission—to establish its position in front. The times we live in cry out for leaders to arise and step forward. *All the more then, my friends, do your utmost to establish that God has called and chosen you. If you do this, you will never stumble....* (2 Peter 1:10, The Revised English Bible). The more familiar King James Version of this verse reads, *Wherefore the rather, brethren, give diligence to make your calling and election sure: for if ye do these things, ye shall never fall.*

Do you have a mission? Do it—even if it looks and sounds radical! Personally, I think it was more than a little *extreme* for two young men to climb up a mountain and take on a whole army. But they did it...and won.

One day I was praying, and I asked the Lord what makes our church in San Antonio, Texas so different? God very plainly spoke to me and said, "Son, the radical spirit you see in your church is part of the beginning of something that I'm doing all across this nation."

The church of the last day will be a church that is absolutely crazy and radical about the God they serve. Its members will go out proclaiming that they are on a mission for God. There's nothing usual, traditional, or conservative about the last-day Benjamin church. *The purpose of leadership is to bring about change.*

God always responds to a person who will take the position of leadership

Jesus Christ did not waste His time looking for lots of people. He came with the strategy to affect twelve lives, and He spent three and a half years, day and night, with these twelve men, making leaders out of followers. The twelve led the seventy-two witnesses. On the day of Pentecost they tarried with 120 who ultimately changed the world.

Jonathan told his army of one, "It's not numbers that we need, because it doesn't matter to God whether He saves by many or by few. All we need to do is lead—do something" (paraphrase of 1 Samuel 14:6).

The Bible says Jonathan and his armor-bearer went up and showed themselves to the Philistines. I imagine it must have gone somewhat like this: "Hey! Over here! Look at us, you uncircumcised fellows! Look at us!"

The Philistines responded, "The Hebrews are coming out of their hiding." They looked down and said, "Come up here so we can teach you a lesson."

Verse 13 says, *Jonathan climbed up, using his hands and feet, with his armor-bearer right behind him.* On their way, he said, "They belong to us. When we get there, we'll take 'em out. Since I'm the leader, I'll knock 'em down, and you take 'em out. We have come to take care of business."

Then he said to the Philistines, "For six years you've intimidated us. My daddy may have backslidden, but I haven't. I'm a Hebrew of Hebrews from the tribe of Benjamin. There's something in me that's slightly radical. Do I look a little crazy? That's because I am. This is my armor-bearer. He follows me. And after him, there's a whole lot more. We're getting ready to kick you all over the desert!"

The Bible says Jonathan and his armor-bearer began to pursue the Philistines. Verse 14 says, *In that first attack Jonathan and his armor-bearer killed some twenty men in an area of about half an acre.*

They were two somewhat crazy young men killing Philistines. They ran around killing Philistines until—verse 15 says—*...the ground shook.* Why did the ground shake? Because when a Benjamite gets going, God gets going. God stepped down with two big feet, and the whole earth started shaking!

One of the Philistines asked, "How many are there?" Another replied, "I don't know, there must be a million or the ground wouldn't shake like this."

"How many do you see?"

"I only see two."

"Two? There has to be more than two."

The next thing you know, the Philistines are arguing among themselves. Verse 20 says, *They found the Philistines in total confu-*

sion, striking each other with their swords. They turned on each other. Why? It all started when somebody dared to stand up and lead.

If you will stand up, God will stand up

If you will run, God will run. If you will lead, God will lead you. When somebody starts leading, even those who have been hiding will come out. They were just waiting on somebody to lead them in the first place. There are people right now who are waiting on you to go crazy in carrying out your mission so they can be released to do the same.

Do you realize that somebody else's deliverance could depend on you taking action? Benjamites are leaders.

> YOU WERE BORN TO HAVE DOMINION. IF ANYBODY IN THE WORLD SHOULD BE LEADING, IT SHOULD BE SANCTIFIED, BLOOD-BOUGHT, HOLY GHOST-FILLED, IN-THEIR-RIGHT-MIND BELIEVERS.

You were born to have dominion. If anybody in the world should be leading, it should be sanctified, blood-bought, Holy Ghost-filled, in-their-right-mind believers. There should be Christian people out in the front saying, "This is the way."

I'm tired of seeing Christians walking around apologizing for living, like we're the weird people in the world. We're not weird—we're leading people to the place they're supposed to go. Don't be confused about who you are.

You should be able to say, "I know exactly who I am, and I know exactly where I'm going. Follow me. I'm a Benjamite."

5

The Benjamin Greeting

When you come to visit my church, Family Praise Center in San Antonio, very likely someone will greet you by saying, "Success to you and success to the Kingdom." That greeting is a quote from my book, *David's Mighty Men*. "Success to you and success to the Kingdom" is not just a flippant phrase. It means, "Blessings unto you. When you wake up in the morning, may you be blessed. May you walk through the whole day with the anointing of God all over you. And when you go to bed tonight, may restful, sweet sleep come to you. Success to you in your work in God's kingdom. I support you and join with you."

Where did this powerful practice begin? It started in Genesis 12:1: *The Lord had said to Abram, "Leave your country, your people and your father's household and go to the land I will show you. I will make you into a great nation and I will bless you; I will make your name great, and you will be a blessing. I will bless those who bless you, and whoever curses you I will curse; and all peoples on earth will be blessed through you."*

The Benjamite apostle, Paul, was a prolific letter writer, and he was really into using salutations that bestowed a blessing. Take a look—

> *Grace and peace to you from God our Father and the Lord Jesus Christ, who gave himself for our sins to rescue us from the present evil age, according to the will of our God and Father, to whom be glory for ever and ever. Amen.*
>
> —Galatians 1:3-5

Grace and peace to you from God our Father and the Lord Jesus Christ. Praise be to the God and Father of our Lord Jesus Christ, who has blessed us in the heavenly realms with every spiritual blessing in Christ.

—Ephesians 1:2,3

Grace and peace to you from God our Father and the Lord Jesus Christ. I thank my God every time I remember you. In all my prayers for all of you, I always pray with joy because of your partnership in the gospel from the first day until now, being confident of this, that he who began a good work in you will carry it on to completion until the day of Christ Jesus.

—Philippians 1:2-6

...Grace and peace to you from God our Father. We always thank God, the Father of our Lord Jesus Christ, when we pray for you, because we have heard of your faith in Christ Jesus and of the love you have for all the saints—the faith and love that spring from the hope that is stored up for you in heaven and that you have already heard about in the word of truth, the gospel that has come to you....

—Colossians 1:2-6

Although I mention only a few of the apostle Paul's greetings to the churches he established, look up his greetings in the books of Romans, Corinthians, and Thessalonians to receive a further blessing. How would you like to be greeted this way every time somebody shook your hand? "Grace be unto you and peace from God the Father and the Lord Jesus Christ." Isn't that a little bit better than, "What's up?"

Greetings are important, and bearers of the Benjamin blessing realize the importance of the words we speak over others. When you say, "Grace be unto you…" you are speaking something important. You're saying, "I want to tell you, God's got your back. Everything's going to be all right. You are covered. I'm praying for you. I'm with you. Amazing grace, how sweet the sound. Grace be unto you."

> *"…GOD'S GOT YOUR BACK!"*

Paul even gives salutations in his benedictions, so he blesses you when he first sees you, and he blesses you again when he leaves. Look them up for yourself in the New Testament.

The way we speak to people is important. When you go for a job interview with your head hanging down, and nonchalantly say, "I was just wondering if you all are taking applications," or "I don't suppose you're hiring," the manager's going to look around and say, "No." *How* you say *what* you say determines the type of response you will receive.

Again, I quote the Benjamite, Paul, in his letter to the Colossians, *Use your heads as you live and work among outsiders. Don't miss a trick. Make the most of every opportunity. Be gracious in your speech. The goal is to bring out the best in others in a conversation, not put them down, not cut them out* (Colossians 4:5,6 The Message).

When you observe the life of Jesus, it soon becomes apparent that He always operated with a calm and peaceful spirit. He was never harsh or hard, arrogant or proud. Even in the hours of trial just prior to the crucifixion, Jesus never lost His temper or attempted to defend Himself. The exact

> YOU ARE A BLESSED BENJAMITE, AND YOU WERE BLESSED TO BE A BLESSING.

opposite was true of His accusers. Some of them reacted violently toward Him—even to the point of screaming curses at Him and throwing things. The crowds *reacted* while Jesus *responded*. Do you see the difference?

You must begin to realize who you are. You are a blessed Benjamite, and you were blessed to be a blessing. That company needs you. You're walking with the grace, peace, and the blessing of God on your life. And wherever there's a born-again, sanctified, blood-bought believer, that place is going to be blessed. Stop apologizing for being a Christian.

Blessed to be a blessing

In Romans 16, Paul makes a point of listing the names of friends who have been a particular blessing to him in his ministry, urging the church in Rome to extend personal greetings to them should they cross paths. He speaks of Phoebe, Priscilla and Aquila, Epenetus, Mary, Andronicus, Junias, and others. He tells the church in Rome, *Greet Apelles, tested and approved in Christ* (v.10). Apelles had probably persevered through some severe trials, resulting in others admiring him for "passing" the tests.

Why this emphasis on greetings? I believe they are used to illustrate that actually exercising true characteristics of the nature of God leads to loving fellowship among people. It also demonstrates that Paul did not esteem himself as greater than other followers of Jesus. Yes, his contribution to the Kingdom exceeds most others. Yes, he was admired as a great church leader. Yet he chose to look upon himself as an equal—simply one of them—a fellow worker for the cause of Christ and a friend to all believers.

In verse 11, Paul mentions Herodion, calling him "my relative." Herodion's name means "my hero." We should always remember those who have played the role of hero in our lives. If anything is lacking in the body of Christ, it's appreciation for one another. Paul didn't want to forget one person who had helped him. And He wanted others to know how helpful these friends had been.

Paul goes on to suggest that believers *greet one another with a holy kiss...* (v.16). There needs to be more kissing going on. You must understand the word *kiss* as it is used in this context. *Phileo*, the Greek word for *kiss* means "to be a friend to; to have affection for (denoting personal attachment); a matter of sentiment or feeling." It can also mean a holy embrace. Here *holy* is translated in the Greek as "physically pure, morally blameless, sacred, and consecrated." It means clean, innocent, modest, and perfect. We need to exercise more freedom in displaying morally blameless affection for one another.

We should slow down when we come in to the church and embrace one another with a *holy phileo*—an embrace accompanied by a physically pure kiss—and speak warm, encouraging words, "Man, I love you. Sister, I love you. Grace be unto you and peace from God our Father and the Lord, Jesus Christ." If you want to be blessed, be a blessing.

"Success to you and success to the Kingdom"

David lived by the principle, "Either greet me right, or you don't get to play on my team." The Benjamites knew how to address David.

> *Other Benjamites...came to David in his stronghold. David went out to meet them and said to them, "If you have come to me in peace, to help me, I am ready to have you unite with me. But if you have come to betray me to my enemies when my hands are free from violence, may the God of our fathers see it and judge you." Then the Spirit came upon Amasai, chief of the Thirty, and he said: "We are yours, O David! We are with you, O son of Jesse! Success, success to you, and success to those who help you, for your God will help you." So David received them and made them leaders of his raiding bands.*
> —1 Chronicles 12:16-18

The King James Version calls *success* "peace." The Hebrew word for *peace* is *shalom,* which means "safe; quiet; well; happy; friendly; prosperous; rest; success; welfare; all is well; salute." So when the Benjamites approached David, he looked at them and asked, "Are you with me?"

Their first words were, "Success to you and success to those who have helped you. We are with you. We are yours, King David."

IT'S TIME FOR YOU TO FALL IN LOVE WITH GOD...

That's loyalty, especially when you realize that David was hiding in a cave during this time. He wasn't a king in his royal palace yet—these Benjamites were giving honor where honor was due *before* they were forced to as a subject of their king.

It's time for you to fall in love with God to the extent that you are not ashamed or embarrassed to display love and affection for all believers in our Savior, Jesus Christ. He is the Lord of all, after all.

When you walk up to someone who knows God's favor is on his life, he is not easily intimidated. Why? He understands the love of God so much that he isn't interested in competition. He just flat out knows his Daddy loves him.

This makes me think about my natural father. He loved me. He's gone to be with Jesus now, but when he was alive, he loved me so much. He'd whip me in a New York second, but he loved me. He would look at me and say, "Ricky, I love you. I'm proud of you." I just swelled up all over when he said that to me.

I remember being knocked down in a football game and running to the sidelines, crying. I was nine or ten years old, playing pee-wee football. My daddy put his hand on my helmet, grabbed my face mask, and said, "Boy, I'm proud of you. I believe in you. But you're not going to come over here and cry to me. Now get in there and knock that boy down."

I said, "Yes, sir!" I went back in the game looking for number sixty-three. I thought, *You just come this way, buddy.* When your father says, "I love you. I believe in you," it makes you confident.

We should bless our children like that. We ought to salute our children this way every day. "Son, I believe in you. You are a man of God." Or, "Girl, you're awesome. You are a blessing in my life." Learn to say, "Kids, I want you to know that you can do anything you want to in life and be successful. You cannot fail."

> I WANT YOU TO KNOW THAT YOU CAN DO ANYTHING YOU WANT TO IN LIFE AND BE SUCCESSFUL. YOU CANNOT FAIL.

Three things children always need to hear are, "I'm proud of you," "I believe in you," and "I love you." The reason many adults are living so pitifully now is because they didn't hear that enough as a child. God is saying to you, "Little Benjamite, I'm proud of you, I believe in you, and I love you. You can do it!"

Man, that's a greeting!

Simply saying, "Here" is no way to serve morning coffee to your spouse. That's no blessing—no salutation or greeting. When you get up in the morning before your spouse, go to the kitchen and make the coffee. Go brush your teeth, comb your hair, and put on a little cologne. Then set a steaming hot cup of coffee on the nightstand, kiss your mate on the forehead, and say, "Baby, I love you. You are the light of my life." Man, that's a greeting!

> REALIZE THE IMPORTANCE OF A POSITIVE, UPLIFTING SALUTATION. IT'S POWERFUL!

Can you even comprehend the results of this type of greeting? Your spouse will get up, drink that coffee, and feel good for the entire day! He or she will go to work feeling loved, appreciated, and blessed. You are blessing your mate. And you're blessing your children when you bless your mate. Realize the importance of a positive, uplifting salutation. It's powerful!

God greeted Abraham well. He said, "I bless you. You're going to be a blessing. Come on out of your house. Come away from your kinfolk. They don't like you anyway. Come with Me. Count these stars. That's how your seed is going to be. Look at this sand here. Can you count all of that?"

"No sir."

"Well, that's how your seed is going to be. You're blessed everywhere you go. You're blessed to be a blessing. I love you so much that I'm going to change your name. From now on you're not Abram but Abraham. It means 'the father of a great multitude.'" What a powerful, significant greeting.

Romans 12:14 says, ...*bless and do not curse.* The word *curse* in this context means "to make someone smaller than they really are." It means to try to make someone believe they are less than God says they are. That's cursing someone. When you tell someone that he or she is less than they really are, you're cursing them. What would happen if we all just changed the way we talked about each other?

Stop talking about people. Stop cursing folks. If you're going to say something, say something good. God told Abraham He would curse anybody who cursed him.

The second meaning of the word *curse* is different. It means "to scorn, to shame, or to bring shame in your life." God was saying, "I'll bitterly curse anyone who tries to make you small or brings you into contempt." I also define it as acting like a snob—you know, a person who flaunts his social superiority or despises those he regards as inferior.

Have you ever walked into a room full of snobs? Don't turn up your nose to your brother, acting like you're better than he is. When you hug your brother you're hugging a world of potential. You'd do yourself a favor to bless your brother. If you get this revelation, it'll change your life.

> *When Israel saw the sons of Joseph, he asked, "Who are these?" "They are the sons God has given me here," Joseph said to his father. Then Israel said, "Bring them to me so I may bless them." Now Israel's eyes were failing because of old age, and he could hardly see. So Joseph brought his sons close to him, and his father kissed them and embraced them.*
>
> —Genesis 48:8-10

God blesses you according to your blessing

You have your own blessing. *You were blessed to be a blessing.* Everything God has spoken about you is success. He doesn't even address the fact that you *might* mess up...that you *might not* succeed. He blesses you according to the potential He sees in you. Benjamite, God talks to you according to the way He has blessed you.

When God looked at Jacob, He saw Israel. When He looked at Ben-oni (birthed in sorrow), he saw Benjamin (the son of His right hand). When He looked at Abram, He saw Abraham, the father of multitudes. When He looked at Simon the fisherman, He saw Peter, the fisher of men. When He looked at Saul of Tarsus, He saw Paul, the apostle, sometimes called "the greatest of Christians and slave and lover of Jesus Christ our Lord." You can be the way God sees you! He never looks at you from the perspective of where you came from or where you are. He always addresses you according to the blessing He has preordained for your life.

What is your *already* blessing?

When God speaks to you, Benjamite, He sees you in a finished state. So you're already blessed, and then He puts a blessing on your blessing. What is your *already* blessing? That God has a preordained plan for your life, and everything about His plan involves your spiritual, physical, emotional, and financial prosperity. Then He crowns it all with a prophecy of success!

GOD HAS A PREORDAINED PLAN FOR YOUR LIFE, AND EVERYTHING ABOUT HIS PLAN INVOLVES YOUR SPIRITUAL, PHYSICAL, EMOTIONAL, AND FINANCIAL PROSPERITY.

When you finally understand this, you will live according to that prophecy, not problems. No matter how bad circumstances appear to be, God says just the opposite. The weapon says it's going to kill you...but God says no weapon formed against you shall prosper (see Isaiah 54:17). Circumstances say you can't make it...but God says you have been equipped to handle every circumstance you'll ever face. Then He gives you favor to make sure it happens. So start smiling! You've got something to be happy about. You're blessed!

I challenge you to start greeting other believers with a smile instead of a frown. "Hello, my brother, grace be unto you and peace. Success to you and success to the kingdom of God." That's powerful. Change the way you talk. Count it all joy. No matter what you're facing, no matter what you're going through, put a smile on your face.

You are a blessing, Benjamin, and you are blessed. Success to you, and success to the Kingdom!

6

A Benjamite Who Would Not Bow

After these events, King Xerxes honored Haman son of Hammedatha, the Agagite, elevating him and giving him a seat of honor higher than that of all the other nobles. All the royal officials at the king's gate knelt down and paid honor to Haman, for the king had commanded this concerning him. But Mordecai would not kneel down or pay him honor. Then the royal officials at the king's gate asked Mordecai, "Why do you disobey the king's command?" Day after day they spoke to him but he refused to comply. Therefore they told Haman about it to see whether Mordecai's behavior would be tolerated, for he had told them he was a Jew.

When Haman saw that Mordecai would not kneel down or pay him honor, he was enraged. Yet having learned who Mordecai's people were, he scorned the idea of killing only Mordecai. Instead Haman looked for a way to destroy all Mordecai's people, the Jews, throughout the whole kingdom of Xerxes.

In the twelfth year of King Xerxes, in the first month, the month of Nisan, they cast the pur (that is, the lot) in the presence of Haman to select a day and month. And the lot fell on the twelfth month, the month of Adar.

Then Haman said to King Xerxes, "There is a certain people dispersed and scattered among the peoples in all the provinces of your kingdom whose customs are different from those of all other people and who do not obey

*the king's laws; it is not in the king's best interest to tol-
erate them. If it pleases the king, let a decree be issued to
destroy them, and I will put ten thousand talents of silver
into the royal treasury for the men who carry out this
business."*

*So the king took his signet ring from his finger and
gave it to Haman son of Hammedatha, the Agagite, the
enemy of the Jews.*

—Esther 3:1-10

If you've ever wondered if God is really involved in the circumstances of your life, perhaps you need to read the Old Testament
book of Esther—a classic narrative of God's character, unfailing
faithfulness to His people, and provision for those who trust Him,
even through events most of us would see as tragic.

Although the author of *Esther* is unknown, most scholars agree
that he was a devout Jew of the tribe of Benjamin who had been carried into exile from Jerusalem by Babylon's King Nebuchadnezzar.
This Benjamite's name was Mordecai.

At this point in our story, many Jews, including Mordecai, had
been released to return to Jerusalem. But Mordecai had chosen to
return to the province of Susa, one of 127 areas ruled by King
Xerxes. It was here that Mordecai left his cousin Esther who, in
keeping with the royal edict, had been taken to the king's palace (see
Esther 2:8) along with other virgins to await Xerxes' call for sexual
favors. She left such a favorable impression on the king, however,
that she became more than a member of the harem and was soon
named Queen of Persia.

Hidden beneath the tapestry of this wonderful story about the
favor of God on a young girl's life is anxiety and concern for the history of Israel. An eternal war was and is raging in the halls of eter-

nity. The enemy's desire to annihilate the people of God is battling against the divine plan of God to deliver and to save His chosen people. So two entities are locked in a battle for the soul of mankind.

Please understand that just as God had a plan for Esther, Mordecai, and the nation of Israel, He also has a plan for you, the bearer of the Benjamin blessing. Ultimately, God's plan involves your victory and success, but Satan also has a plan. And his plan is diametrically opposed to the plan of God for your life. Let us consider a pivotal moment in the preordained, eternal strategy of God as written in the book of Esther.

Every problem has a name and a mission

Every significant problem in your life needs to be measured against God's prophetic will. In other words, every born-again believer can handle any problem in life by challenging his or her situation in light of the prophecy God has already stated in His Word. Problems have names...and also purposes and missions. The mission of many problems you experience is to destroy you or to keep you from your potential. If Satan can keep you from moving forward, he has stolen your destiny.

> IF SATAN CAN KEEP YOU FROM MOVING FORWARD, HE HAS STOLEN YOUR DESTINY.

God knew about every problem in your life before it visited your house. And we believe that, somehow, each problem can be solved in harmony with God's prophecy for your life.

It is hard to defeat any man or woman who truly believes this. Despite a bruise or a knock every now and then, the believer always bounces back because he chooses to believe what God says over what the circumstance says. Ask yourself what the Word says about any problem you're facing. Remember, *...all things God works for* *the good of those who love him, who have been called according to his purpose* (Romans 8:28).

In essence, the people of God in the book of Esther had a problem with a purpose. The problem's name was Haman, and he was being used by the devil to plot the annihilation of the people of God—Satan's purpose from the beginning of all time.

Satan is not only opposed to God's plan for every person's life, but his plan includes creating problems for you that lead to utter destruction. He does not like you!

Fellow Benjamite, you and I are charged to be a problem to Satan and the powers of darkness and evil that prevail in this world, and our mission is to destroy the works of the enemy of our soul. We have important work to do for the kingdom of God. When we set out to deliver the Truth as revealed in God's Word, we can be absolutely certain of one thing—the devil is not going to leave us alone.

> WHEN WE REALIZE THAT GOD SPECIFICALLY DESIGNED US FOR A SPECIAL PURPOSE AND THAT WE'RE IMPORTANT AND SIGNIFICANT, THE DEVIL BECOMES MIGHTY INTERESTED IN US.

When we stop singing, praising, and working for God, we cause no trouble for the devil. But when we realize that God specifically designed us for a special purpose and that we're important and significant, the devil becomes mighty interested in us. When he gets worried, he starts trying to create problems for us. Problems are his specialty.

The enemy always operates in his eternal nature. His nature was revealed in the first prophecy ever given in Scripture, *And I will put enmity between you and the woman, and between your offspring and hers; he will crush your head, and you will strike his heel* (Genesis 3:15). At that point the enemy lived up to his prophetic nature, declaring that he would war against anything initiated from the seed of God.

It is Satan's nature to cause trouble. Someone once said, "If you're not running against the devil, that's a good sign you're walking with him."

If you're experiencing problems unlike any you've ever had, you must be doing something right. If you feel as though every time you try to do something right, the devil hits you, be encouraged! Just go ahead and do it anyway.

A problem named Haman

The book of Esther talks about a problem named Haman. *After these events, King Xerxes honored Haman son of Hammedatha, the Agagite, elevating him and giving him a seat of honor higher than that of all the other nobles* (Esther 3:1). The Agagites were constituents of King Agag of Amalek, whose name means, "I will overcome." The Amalekites were constant enemies of God throughout the Old Testament.

They are first mentioned in the book of Exodus:

> *The Amalekites came and attacked the Israelites at Rephidim. Moses said to Joshua, "Choose some of our men and go out to fight the Amalekites. Tomorrow I will stand on top of the hill with the staff of God in my hands." So Joshua fought the Amalekites as Moses had ordered, and Moses, Aaron and Hur went to the top of the hill. As long as Moses held up his hands, the Israelites were winning, but whenever he lowered his hands, the Amalekites were winning. When Moses' hands grew tired, they took a stone and put it under him and he sat on it. Aaron and*

Hur held his hands up—one on one side, one on the other—so that his hands remained steady till sunset.

—Exodus 17:8-12

Oh, for people of God who will get a spirit of Aaron and Hur—people who will observe somebody having a problem in life and say, "I'm not going to let you lose your praise." You see, as long as your hands are raised, you win. You cannot be conquered when you maintain an attitude of praise. Your hands represent praise, production, and power. When your hands come down, you lose.

Shout for joy to the Lord, all the earth. Worship the Lord with gladness; come before him with joyful songs. Know that the Lord is God. It is he who made us, and we are his; we are his people, the sheep of his pasture. Enter his gates with thanksgiving and his courts with praise; give thanks to him and praise his name. For the Lord is good and his love endures forever; his faithfulness continues through all generations.

—Psalm 100:1-5

We need brothers and sisters to come alongside us and say, "I know you're going through some rough times right now, and you don't feel like praising God. But I'm here to help you, and I refuse to let your hands come down. As a matter of fact, just take a seat and I'll lift up your hands for you. You're not going to lose your praise!"

Praise kept Abraham strong in spite of the years that had passed since God had deposited a promise in him. Romans 4:20,21 say, *Yet he* [Abraham] *did not waver through unbelief regarding the promise of God, but was strengthened in his faith and gave glory to God, being fully persuaded that God had power to do what he had promised.* Praise releases joy and honors God. We ought to praise Him, then, for that reason alone!

We need to have a bulldog determination to praise God *anyway*—no matter what problem, situation, or circumstances we encounter!

> *So Joshua overcame the Amalekite army with the sword. Then the Lord said to Moses, "Write this on a scroll as something to be remembered and make sure that Joshua hears it, because I will completely blot out the memory of Amalek from under heaven." Moses built an altar and called it The Lord is my Banner. He said, "For hands were lifted up to the throne of the Lord. The Lord will be at war against the Amalekites from generation to generation."*
>
> —Exodus 17:13-16

God said He would be against the Amalekites from generation to generation to generation. Amalek represents the problems of intimidation, rulership, and domination. But God is against any spiritual force that sets itself against His people. He is determined to annihilate it once and for all, forever.

The very first enemy the Israelites faced when they came out of Egypt was the Amalekites. God's people came out from under the iron hand of Pharaoh only to meet the Amalekites—the spirit of intimidation.

How many times have you walked in freedom and victory on Sunday, only to wake up on Monday morning to face the threats of the devil—"I don't care what you did Sunday, honey, you are now back in my control. When I tell you to sin, you're going to sin. When I tell you to submit, you're going to submit."

Well, God said, "I am after that spirit that comes after my people *every time* they are delivered."

Don't let your hands get tired, Benjamin. God is after the Amalekite in your life. He's after the Haman in your life. Today you will be set free, and you'll walk over Amalek tomorrow.

The next mention of the Amalekites is in 1 Samuel 14:47,48, *After Saul had assumed rule over Israel, he fought against their enemies on every side: Moab, the Ammonites, Edom, the kings of Zobah, and the Philistines. Wherever he turned, he inflicted punishment on them. He fought valiantly and defeated the Amalekites, delivering Israel from the hands of those who had plundered them.*

If 1 Samuel 15 had never been written, we would still be shouting, but something horrible transpired in that next chapter. The prophet Samuel came to Saul with a word from the Lord—wipe out the Amalekites, no ifs, ands, or buts! But the Bible says that Saul grabbed the Amalekite king, Agag, and did not kill him as God had instructed. And he kept the best of the sheep, oxen, and everything that looked good.

First Samuel 15:17-19 says, *"Although you were once small in your own eyes, did you not become the head of the tribes of Israel? The Lord anointed you king over Israel. And he sent you on a mission, saying, 'Go and completely destroy those wicked people, the Amalekites; make war on them until you have wiped them out.' Why did you not obey the Lord? Why did you pounce on the plunder and do evil in the eyes of the Lord?"*

God was simply saying, "Saul, I've been waiting on you to get here. You're a Benjamite. You walk in the blessing of Benjamin. I told you to make war against the Amalekites until they disappeared from the face of the earth. Why didn't you obey Me? Why did you take their *stuff* and do evil in My eyes? Why didn't you do as I said, Saul?"

Time and again, people run to the altar in pursuit of an emotional experience and swat at the enemy, but they don't take him out.

It's time to stop playing games with your problem. Tell your problem, whatever it is—habits, hobbies, self-worth, depression, gossip, fault-finding, complaining, worrying—"Today, I'm not only going to knock you down, but I'm going to take you out. I will not compromise. You will not come near my house, my street, my city, my state, or my nation. It's over as of today!" Benjamites don't negotiate with the devil.

> WHAT WE DON'T DEFEAT NOW IS GOING TO DEFEAT US LATER.

What you don't defeat now will rise up against you later

Throughout the history of the world, man has had a problem whose name is procrastination. A great many people today live with an escapist mentality that believes their problems will eventually evaporate and they'll be okay. *"Someday* we'll win," they say. *"Someday* we'll get past this."

Here's a news flash! *Someday* is never going to come. What we don't defeat now is going to defeat us later. We have to make up our mind and say, "Enough is enough. I'm not taking anymore. Devil, you're going out this day."

Saul had a problem whose name was disobedience. He did not kill all the Amalekites as God had instructed him to do, and later on, in 2 Samuel 1:1, we find David returning from defeating them. He never would have had to fight the Amalekites had Saul obeyed God in the first place!

What we don't defeat in our generation, the following generation will have to contend with. For example, the issues of homosexuality and "gay rights" do not intimidate me. It's *not* okay. It's *never* been okay. And it *never will be* okay!

Perhaps you don't agree with me, but I'm telling you that if you're a practicing homosexual, you are living in sin, and you need to get delivered. Homosexuality is not an "alternate lifestyle." Let's call it what it is—sin! If you're sleeping with someone else's wife, you are an adulterous sinner, and you're no better than a homosexual.

If you're lying and stealing from your employer, you're a sinner, period. If you're drinking yourself into oblivion or numbing your senses with drugs (even those prescribed by your physician), you are sinning! If you submit your soul to the sinful nature, described in Galatians 5:19-21 as "sexual immorality, impurity and debauchery; idolatry and witchcraft; hatred, discord, jealousy, fits of rage, selfish orgies, and the like," you won't inherit the kingdom of God. That's the end of the story. There are no degrees of sin—sin is sin.

> WHO WILL STAND UP AND CRY OUT AGAINST SIN?

Who will stand up and cry out against sin? We have a mindset that everything will turn out all right...eventually. We'll take care of it later. No! Let's take care of it right now, because I don't want my son or my daughters to have to deal with stuff that I didn't defeat.

David had to fight the Amalekites because Saul hadn't dealt with them when he should have. Look at what happened:

> *On the third day a man arrived from Saul's camp, with his clothes torn and with dust on his head. When he came to David, he fell to the ground to pay him honor. "Where have you come from?" David asked him. He answered, "I have escaped from the Israelite camp." "What happened?" David asked. "Tell me." He said, "The men fled from the battle. Many of them fell and died. And Saul and his son Jonathan are dead." Then David said to the young man who brought him the report, "How do you know that Saul and his son Jonathan are dead?"*

"I happened to be on Mount Gilboa," the young man said, "and there was Saul, leaning on his spear, with the chariots and riders almost upon him. When he turned around and saw me, he called out to me, and I said, 'What can I do?'

"He asked me, 'Who are you?' "'An Amalekite,' I answered. "Then he said to me, 'Stand over me and kill me! I am in the throes of death, but I'm still alive.' "So I stood over him and killed him, because I knew that after he had fallen he could not survive. And I took the crown that was on his head and the band on his arm and have brought them here to my lord."

—2 Samuel 1:2-10

What Saul did not annihilate came back to annihilate him...and his beloved son Jonathan. It didn't have to be that way. This generation of churchgoers has been sold a passive philosophy of stepping our way to deliverance—we call it "rehabilitation." There are twelve-step programs for every imaginable condition. Let me tell you—when a vampire bat is fastened on my neck sucking out my lifeblood, I don't want to pull it off a little step at a time! This generation needs a radical move of God's Spirit to show them that they don't have to remain deceived by a lie of the enemy.

The Benjamin-blessed generation says, "In Jesus' name, I can change *right now.*" Benjamites don't bow.

Back to our Bible history. Five hundred years later, after Saul failed to stamp out and totally destroy the Amalekites, Haman, the Amalekite, is doing what Amalekites always do—intimidating and destroying the people of God.

Then Haman said to King Xerxes, "There is a certain people dispersed and scattered among the peoples in

all the provinces of your kingdom whose customs are dif-
ferent from those of all other people and who do not obey
the king's laws; it is not in the king's best interest to tol-
erate them. If it pleases the king, let a decree be issued to
destroy them, and I will put ten thousand talents of silver
into the royal treasury for the men who carry out this
business."

So the king took his signet ring from his finger and
gave it to Haman son of Hammedatha, the Agagite, the
enemy of the Jews. "Keep the money," the king said to
Haman, "and do with the people as you please."

Then on the thirteenth day of the first month the
royal secretaries were summoned. They wrote out in the
script of each province and in the language of each peo-
ple all Haman's orders to the king's satraps, the gover-
nors of the various provinces and the nobles of the vari-
ous peoples. These were written in the name of King
Xerxes himself and sealed with his own ring. Dispatches
were sent by couriers to all the king's provinces with the
order to destroy, kill and annihilate all the Jews—young
and old, women and little children—on a single day....

—Esther 3:8-13

Benjamites don't fit in this world. If you're not different from
the world, something is wrong with you. At some point we've got to
get a Shadrach, Meshach and Abednego spirit that refuses to bow to
the world's ways. Haman's unreasonable rage against Mordecai
stemmed directly from Mordecai's refusal to submit.

Except for Mordecai, all the royal officials knelt daily at the
king's gate to pay honor to Haman in obedience to King Xerxes'
decree. Every day that Mordecai ignored the royal decree incensed
Haman more.

But Mordecai wasn't intimidated. He just looked at Haman. I can imagine him saying something like this: "I'm a Benjamite, and I don't bow. Everyone else might bow, but I won't bow to your destruction. I won't bow to your rage. I won't submit to your intimidation. I'll look at you eye-to-eye. Every day I'm going to stand right here in your gate and look at you, but I'm not going to bow."

God's people cannot continue sinning Monday through Saturday, then sit in the pew, sing on the praise team, or greet at the door of the church on Sunday, and say everything's going to be all right. It's not going to be all right.

I realize this is not a popular approach, but God is still a God of holiness, high standards, and convictions. He says sin is sin and holiness is holiness, and that's it! I refuse to bow to the pressure of society.

According to Isaiah 54:17, *"No weapon forged against you* [we Benjamites] *will prevail, and you* [we Benjamites] *will refute every tongue that accuses you* [us]. *This is the heritage of the servants of the Lord, and this is their vindication from me," declares the Lord.* The devil's problems of opposition will not succeed. But we, as believers, have to get it together and declare that sin is sin, righteousness is righteousness, and that's how it is. You can't hate your brother and go to heaven. You cannot live a gay lifestyle and go to heaven. You cannot live an adulterous lifestyle and go to heaven. You can't indulge in pornography and go to heaven. You can't do it!

Some "Mordecais" of the tribe of Benjamin have to stand up and say, "I've got a Shadrach, Meshach, and Abednego spirit in me. Throw me in the fiery furnace. I would rather burn than bow. But I'm not bowing."

Christ is raising up a chosen generation
This generation has been waiting for you and me to step into

our places. This generation was tailor-made for us. What am I saying? I'm saying you can't catch God off guard. We are eternally positioned by Christ.

THIS GENERATION HAS BEEN WAITING FOR YOU AND ME TO STEP INTO OUR PLACES. WE ARE ETERNALLY POSITIONED BY CHRIST.

On March 11, 1961, God said, "Rick Hawkins, come forth. I have a generation that is waiting on you." This is my generation. I am responsible for it. Before the world began, God knew I'd be born when I was born. He saw me preaching and writing this message for you.

He saw you reading this book, arming yourself with vital information to equip you to take your position on the front lines in the eternal battle for the end-time harvest. He saw an integrated army of Benjamites arising all over this nation, people who love Him and are radical about His purpose for their lives.

This is our generation. Before there was sin, there was sacrifice. Before there was a flood, there was an ark. Before there was sickness, there were stripes. Before there was brokenness, there was restoration. Before there was a Haman, there was a Mordecai. Before there was a problem, there was a prophecy. Before there was a Goliath, there was a David. Before there was a generation called "X," there was a Benjamite.

David served the purpose of God in his own generation, and then he fell asleep. He owned his generation. Until we take ownership of our generation, we will have more gang violence, more gay marches, and more sin in the church. Until we take ownership in this generation and say, "No, Benjamites do not bow—this is our generation and we will live holy," we will not possess our land.

Purpose means everything. Everything in your life rises and falls on your purpose. The reason pastors have such a hard time getting together is because we're threatened—we're scared. What a we scared of? Competition. Thus we have churches working to see who can draw the biggest crowd, have the most busses, build the plushest building, and raise the most money! Competition is a sickness!

Understanding your purpose eliminates the need for competition and all concern about your position. Competitors in ministry are men and women who do not know who they are—local churches made up of driven competitors who don't know the "why" of being.

> UNDERSTANDING YOUR PURPOSE ELIMINATES THE NEED FOR COMPETITION AND ALL CONCERN ABOUT YOUR POSITION.

We must get back to our purpose and foundation and discover why in the world we were born...why we are here.

God is never without a servant...never without a plan

Queen Esther was a Benjamitess. But when asked to intercede with the king for her people, the Jews, she was afraid. She sent word to her Uncle Mordecai saying, "I can't do what you want me to do because it's against the law" (my paraphrase).

> *When Esther's words were reported to Mordecai, he sent back this answer: "Do not think that because you are in the king's house you alone of all the Jews will escape. For if you remain silent at this time, relief and deliverance for the Jews will arise from another place, but you and your father's family will perish. And who knows but that you have come to royal position for such a time as this?"*
> —Esther 4:12-14

somebody waiting. In case you are disobedi-ed plan of God in your life, don't think that God is defeated and in a frenzy, because He has somebody else waiting in the wings. Mordecai said, "Esther, if you don't do your job, somebody's going to do it for you. You'd better rise up like a myrtle tree—like your name says you are."

> ...O
> ...AT IN
> CASE ...U DON'T
> ANSWER HIS CALL,
> HE'S PREPARED TO
> FIND SOMEONE WHO
> WILL. DON'T LET
> SOMEONE ELSE TAKE
> YOUR PLACE.

A myrtle tree grows in muddy places and produces fragrance in her flowers. You may be in a mess today, but you can grow. It may be muddy around you, but you can grow. Your bills may not be paid, but you can grow right there.

Your family may be falling apart, but you can give off a fragrance right where you are. It may be difficult and unpleasant all around you, but you can produce.

Mordecai told Esther, "If you don't do this, relief and deliverance will come...." The word *deliverance* there literally means "respiration." I tell you, Benjamite, God's people will breathe again. He wants to use you, but in case you don't answer His call, He's prepared to find someone who will. Don't let someone else take your place.

> *Then Esther sent this reply to Mordecai: "Go, gather together all the Jews who are in Susa, and fast for me. Do not eat or drink for three days, night or day. I and my maids will fast as you do. When this is done, I will go to the king, even though it is against the law. And if I perish, I perish." So Mordecai went away and carried out all of Esther's instructions.*

—vv. 15-17

Say to yourself, "I'm about to do something. I'm changing things. I'm not going to sit around anymore. I'm not just going to sit on my chair. I'm not going to just take it as it comes, but I'm about to get up and do something."

ALL YOU HAVE TO DO IS MAKE UP YOUR MIND THAT YOU WON'T BOW.

Your eternal position does not nullify your responsibility to your generation. You're not here because you look good. The work that we're doing is not done inside the church house—it's done in the world. We go to church to prepare us to take the message to the world. We're in church getting made up. We're just getting equipped inside—but the work is outside. Don't forget why you're here.

It's always tempting to try and evade responsibility. We don't like anyone telling us that we have a responsibility to our generation. Mordecai reminded Esther of who she was. He said, "You are also a Jew."

Don't forget who you are. You are also a Benjamite. You are a chosen generation. The next time someone asks you who you are, tell them, "I am a chosen generation, a royal priesthood, a holy nation. I am a peculiar person. I will show forth the praises of Him who called me out of darkness into His marvelous light. That's my responsibility, and I don't need anyone else to take my place. I plan on doing a good job of it myself."

The Bible says that the gallows Haman built for the destruction of the Jews was used to hang him. The very thing the devil is trying to use against you may be used to destroy his work. Whatever the devil is doing against you is going to turn against him. All you have to do is make up your mind that you won't bow.

You are a part of the Benjamin blessing.

7

A Benjamin Beneath the Stuff

Now there was a man of Benjamin, whose name was Kish...a mighty man of power. And he had a son, whose name was Saul, a choice young man, and a goodly: and there was not among the children of Israel a goodlier person than he: from his shoulders and upward he was higher than any of the people.

When [Samuel] had caused the tribe of Benjamin to come near by their families, the family of Matri was taken, and Saul the son of Kish was taken: and when they sought him, he could not be found. Therefore they inquired of the Lord further, if the man should yet come thither. And the Lord answered, Behold, he hath hid himself among the stuff. And they ran and fetched him thence....

—1 Samuel 9:1,2; 10:21-23 KJV

First and Second Samuel provide a history of Israel and its leaders from the end of the Judges to David's waning years—a period of about 100 years. The aging prophet Samuel had produced no suitable heirs to take his place, providing a ready-made excuse for the people to demand a king, wanting to be like the nations surrounding them. Although Samuel warned them of the cost—pointing out that neighboring countries were subject to forced labor, taxation, and loss of personal freedom—the people remained unmoved.

Of all the people of Israel, God led Samuel to seek a tall and handsome Benjamite named Saul to fill the position. But when it came time for the private anointing ceremony, Saul was nowhere to be found because he was hiding...among the stuff.

You may run, but you cannot hide

God is used to people hiding from Him. Moses had tried to hide from God behind a stammering tongue, and God responded, "I don't need your mouth, son, I'm only interested in your heart."

Esther had tried to hide behind her royal position when the threat of imminent execution of the Jews presented itself. Then her uncle, the Benjamite, Mordecai, approached Esther, saying, "How do you know that you weren't born for this purpose?"

Gideon hid in the threshing floor trying to get away from the call of God. Jeremiah, trying to hide behind his youth, asked, "Who will listen to me? I'm just a child!" God said, "I'm not interested in your excuses. I'll put My words in your mouth." Rebelling against God's commission to preach repentance to Nineveh, the reluctant missionary Jonah decided to take a cruise to get away from God. He wound up in the belly of a sea monster!

It doesn't matter where you're hiding or what kind of *stuff* you have piled on top of you when God says, "Now is your time." He isn't interested in your excuses, and He always knows where to find you.

Maybe they'll look for someone else...

Why would Saul run from God? I believe he felt unworthy and unprepared for the job and was afraid of the responsibility. He thought if they couldn't find him they would choose someone else.

Sound familiar? Let's explore these areas and try to identify why you are where you find yourself today. If you've been hiding from a mandate of God on your life, I've written this book to tell you, in the words of an old song, to "come out of that corner…you can't hide."

God often chooses people who say, "I can't do it." Like Saul, you may have feelings of inadequacy. Many people refuse to stand up and get into the place where God has called them because they don't want to fail or look foolish. They're afraid of becoming vulnerable to the opinions of others. Remember, it's not about you—but about the God in you.

It's time for men and women of God to cultivate a Benjamite spirit that says, "I might fall, but I'll still lead. If I fall, I'll get back up, dust myself off, and keep on going. You can't stop me!" God has called you to face the Philistines and the Ammonites of our day. He has called you to stand up and say, "This generation belongs to me. I'm not afraid to address issues in this hour."

> GOD OFTEN CHOOSES PEOPLE WHO SAY, "I CAN'T DO IT."

It's time to stand and prophesy to your problems. If your spouse starts nagging and complaining, just look at him or her and prophesy, "No weapon, baby, formed against us shall prosper." Stand up and lead.

What kind of stuff do you have?

Saul hid himself among the stuff. What kind of stuff do you have? The word *hid* expresses the idea of covering up or doing things in secret. Lots of people are hiding behind their secrets. You never let anyone know something's wrong because it's your secret. At the same time, you refuse to get out in front because you know what you've got covered up.

So we hide behind *stuff*—we use *stuff* as an excuse to avoid facing up to our "hidden" problems. Do you have a secret that you think nobody knows?

Have you become dependent on habits that control your actions? Is it more comfortable to worry, gossip, procrastinate, drink a beer, or smoke a joint than it is to turn to the Word of God and prayer? Is it easier to run to the mall and shop until you drop than it is to set aside a quiet time to enter into the presence of God and let Him clear away the fog?

Have you settled for less than God's best for you because it's easier...because your comfort zone is so well furnished that you can't even stand to think of the upheaval of remodeling? God is calling His people to live by principle, not preference—to live by conviction, not convenience. God wants to deal with your stuff!

> GOD IS CALLING HIS PEOPLE TO LIVE BY PRINCIPLE, NOT PREFERENCE— TO LIVE BY CONVICTION, NOT CONVENIENCE. GOD WANTS TO DEAL WITH YOUR STUFF!

He wants you and me to stomp on our eating, shopping, smoking, drinking, pill-popping addictions and make a firm decision to leave them in the past. Stop hiding behind the victim mentality that says, "I am a victim. I am this way because of my parents...the color of my skin...my lack of education...." *Stop that!* Square your shoulders and say, "I know exactly who I am, where I came from, and where I'm going. I'm not a victim of anything. I am a victor through Jesus Christ my Savior."

Perhaps you are hiding behind your past, feeling that something you did years ago disqualifies you for what God has anointed you to do. *If you're going to live with condemnation from your past, then welcome to your future.* No one has qualified you to do what you're supposed to do but God Himself.

How long will you allow your past to separate you from God's call? It is your decision alone that can keep your past from determining your future. Thank God for His forgiveness, mercy, and grace! You can trust Him with your yesterdays. Give your past to

God. Do you know what He'll do with it? Hebrews 10:16,17 AMP says, *This is the agreement (testament, covenant) that I will set up and conclude with them after those days, says the Lord: I will imprint My laws upon their hearts, and I will inscribe them on their minds (on their inmost thoughts, and understanding), He then goes on to say, And their sins and their lawbreaking I will remember no more.* He'll forget all about it...if you stop reminding Him of it.

Nobody said it would be easy

When you make the decision to leave your past in the past, it is highly likely that someone who was close to you in those days (who knows everything about you because they were there) will come out of the woodwork, saying things like, "Who do you think you are? I know what you were like before. I was there when you did this or that."

That happened when Samuel announced that Saul would be Israel's king. First Samuel 10:27 KJV says, *But the children of Belial said, How shall this man save us? And they despised him, and brought him no presents. But he held his peace.*

There will always be someone who says, "I know about you. I know what you did." The name *Belial* literally means "worthlessness." You need to confront that worthless spirit and say, "You're a lying devil. You're wicked."

I'm convinced that the devil will assign people to try and destroy you. They'll never let you forget your past. That being the case, just cut those negative relationships off and move on. Don't worry about what they're saying. It's only what God says that matters anyway. Follow Saul's example. The Bible says, "he held his peace." Saul didn't even respond.

Right now, you may be trying to do right, but your friends and family keep reminding you that they know where you're from and what you've done. Don't respond to them. The truth is, they don't know where you came from. They don't know how you cried last night. They don't know how those chains were broken off of your life.

Psalm 103 lists the benefits to be enjoyed from your relationship with the Lord. It is especially helpful to recall the mercies of God when you're dealing with those who won't let you forget your past. The list begins in verse 3: God forgives all your sins, heals all your diseases, redeems your life from destruction, crowns you with love and compassion, satisfies your desires with good things, renews your youth, works righteousness and justice when you're oppressed, makes His ways known to you, and gives you His grace and mercy when you need them (my paraphrase).

As if that weren't enough, verses 11 and 12 say this: *For as high as the heavens are above the earth, so great is his love for those who fear him; as far as the east is from the west, so far has he removed our transgressions from us.* Granted, this is a metaphor. But think about it. *When the Lord removes your sins, they no longer exist anywhere!*

God can find you

"Where is he?"

"I don't know, we can't find him."

"Well, this man's supposed to be appointed king today. Did y'all check over here?"

"Look at all this stuff. He's got to be in here somewhere. Where is he?"

"Saul? Saul? Saul?"

"Where is he?"

"Lord, we can't find him."

God knew where Saul was hiding, and He can find you too. You say, "I can't do it, God. I'm not ready. I've got stuff to deal with. As soon as I give it up I'll get back to you, God." Or, "I'm inadequate. I don't have the potential. I'll never feel worthy. I've tried, but I just couldn't make it." Or, "I've tried to quit worrying, but I can't. I don't want to be depressed, but I am." "I don't want to drink and look at pornographic magazines, but I can't help it." Stuff! God knows exactly where you are.

> I LEFT YOU IN DOMINION. I LEFT YOU MULTIPLYING AND INCREASING IN NUMBER.

God called, "Adam, Adam, where are you, son?" (see Genesis 3:9). Do you really think God didn't know where Adam was? He's all-knowing and all-powerful, and He knew exactly where Adam was. God was merely asking, "Where are you in relation to the condition I left you in? I left you in dominion. I left you multiplying and increasing in number. I left you keeping a garden. I left you protecting a wife."

> *O Lord, you have searched me [thoroughly] and have known me. You know my downsitting and my uprising; You understand my thought afar off. You sift and search out my path and my lying down, and You are acquainted with all my ways. For there is not a word in my tongue [still unuttered], but, behold, O Lord, You know it altogether. You have beset me and shut me in—behind and before, and You have laid Your hand upon me. Your [infinite] knowledge is too wonderful for me; it is high above me, I cannot reach it. Where could I go from Your Spirit? Or where could I flee from Your presence? If I ascend up into heaven, You are there; if I make my bed in Sheol (the place of the dead), behold, You are there. If I take the wings of the morning or dwell in the uttermost parts of the sea, even there shall Your hand lead me, and Your right hand shall hold me.*
>
> —Psalm 139:1-10 AMP

God is for you and not against you. Verse 16 of that Psalm goes on to say, *Your eyes saw my unformed substance, and in Your book all the days [of my life] were written before ever they took shape, when as yet there was none of them.* The word *substance* means "power" and "potential."

God saw something in you even when you were trying to hide from Him. You tried to crawl under all the stuff you had accumulated, but God saw you...and saw something in you that He wouldn't leave alone.

God has an agenda

God is after one thing—fulfillment of the purpose He pre-ordained for your life—your destiny. He has one agenda concerning you—that you do and be all that He has purposed for you to do and be. When people give up on you and you're buried beneath all kinds of stuff, God is still looking for your substance. There's more to you than what you see. The anointing of God is able to shatter the image you've built of yourself.

> GOD IS AFTER ONE THING— FULFILLMENT OF THE PURPOSE HE PRE-ORDAINED FOR YOUR LIFE— YOUR DESTINY.

You may find yourself on the verge of giving up today. You may have piled lots of stuff around you to keep your potential hidden. There is a lot of good work undone and ministry gifts lying dormant because of stuff.

Perhaps you have reached a certain level where you feel okay about yourself. Well, welcome to your future—because this is it. If you've started letting stuff get involved with the position you inhabit, you can't go any further. You've reached the "ceiling" because there's too much stuff (compromise and mediocrity) piled on top of you. Don't measure yourself by those around you, but by the potential God has given you to become.

Until you get the stuff out, you're not going anywhere. You'll never write that book, you'll never sing that song, you'll never preach that message—but God is never going to leave you alone. He knows where you're hiding.

Benjamin, come out from under the stuff!

Our national consciousness wasn't outraged by the allegations of wrongdoing in the Clinton White House in the late '90s. No! In fact, we chose to look the other way. Why? I think many people were so impure themselves that they didn't want attention focused on blatant, outright sin. God help us! We're in trouble. Benjamin, come out from under the stuff of compromise!

There was a day in the history of this country when its leaders never would have put up with the immoral and unjust acts that are now tolerated and casually accepted. Our forefathers were men of God who would have said, "We're going to bring this out into the open, and we're going to clean it up. We must keep moving forward. We have a destiny to fulfill...and these issues will not be ignored!"

> THERE IS TOO MUCH STUFF, AND IT'S BECAUSE WE'VE DECIDED TO LIVE BY WHAT WE PREFER AND NOT BY THE PRINCIPLES GOD HAS ESTABLISHED.

The church has also lowered its standards. Nobody seems to care about the sin that tries to make itself at home in the house of God. Our actions say, "Oh, of course you can be on the worship team. You drink and smoke? You live with some guy who won't marry you? That's all right, baby—we don't want to offend you. Please sing." Not in my church! Take your song down the street to the barroom, where you can sing for drinks.

Folks don't want to hear that because they love their sin too much. We excuse sin and sit passively by. No one wants to raise a standard in this hour for fear they'll lose someone who might bring a big offering.

God is still holy, and He's looking for a holy people. I believe in mercy, and I'm all for working things through with people. But, it seems, the more you work with people and their addictions, the more people abuse you.

Our teenagers have sex, and pastors sit back and say, "Oh, well, they're just kids." What kind of a thing is that? Stuff! Marriages are falling apart because both spouses are acting crazy …and many are on the verge of divorce. More stuff! There is too much stuff, and it's because we've decided to live by what we prefer and not by the principles God has established.

A spirit of compromise has been unleashed on the church. You say, "How do you know, Pastor?" Because some Christians are allowing their kids to watch unbelievable things on television— nudity, violence, obscenity, murder—overlooking it because they don't want them to leave home. That's *stuff*. The reason it isn't addressed is because the parents are involved in it too!

God is calling for a clean church. He is saying, "I'm not going to tolerate your sin. I'm not going to permit your stuff. I know where you are. Your friends may not know what you're doing, but I know. Your family may not know what you're up to, but I know. You're hiding beneath your stuff, and it's time to get the stuff out!"

True Benjamites will lead the last-day church. *Benjamin* means "the son of my right hand." Further, it suggests leadership that is warlike in its approach to the end-time harvest—radical, unorthodox, non-traditional…with an insatiable appetite for righteousness. In this last day, God is calling forth a remnant—people who believe a firestorm of the Holy Ghost is coming that will burn up the *stuff* in people's lives as it passes by, resulting in complete intolerance for compromise.

When Samuel called out Saul's family from the tribe of Benjamin to find Israel's king, he first called Saul's grandfather, Matri. His name means "he of the rain" or "it's about to rain." Saul's father's name was Kish, which means "to set a trap" or "to lay a snare."

In this last day, God is strategically constructing a trap for the enemy. We are about to hit the devil with something he's not expecting. I'm tired of seeing the church get caught. I'm ready to see the enemy ensnared in the tangled web of deception he has woven over the centuries. How about you?

Benjamite, come out from under the stuff and say, "Devil, Benjamin is here, and you're busted!"

8

O Benjamin, Be on Your Guard!

I know Ephraim, and Israel is not hid from Me; for now, O Ephraim, you have played the harlot and have worshiped idols; Israel is defiled. Their doings will not permit them to return to their God, for the spirit of harlotry is within them and they know not the Lord [they do not recognize, appreciate, give heed to, or cherish the Lord].

But the pride and self-reliance of Israel testifies before his [own] face. Therefore shall [all] Israel, and [especially] Ephraim [the northern ten tribes], totter and fall in their iniquity and guilt, and Judah shall stumble and fall with them. They shall go with their flocks and with their herds to seek the Lord [inquiring for and requiring Him], but they will not find Him; He has withdrawn Himself from them. They have dealt faithlessly and treacherously with the Lord [their espoused Husband], for they have borne alien children. Now shall a [single] New Moon (one month) devour them with their fields. Blow the horn in Gibeah and the trumpet in Ramah [both lofty hills on Benjamin's northern borders]. Sound the alarm at Beth-aven: [the enemy is] behind you and after you, O Benjamin [be on your guard]!

—Hosea 5:3-8 AMP

In the New International Version, verse 8 says, *"Sound the trumpet in Gibeah, the horn in Ramah. Raise the battle cry in Beth Aven; lead on, O Benjamin."*

There is much to consider here. At the core of his prophecy, Hosea includes Benjamin in unfolding God's eternal plan for His people. God's people were in trouble. They had turned to prostitution (harlotry). They had been unfaithful and were full of infidelity.

Hosea would say they were *flaky*—they had served God at one time, but now had wandered astray and found themselves infatuated with serving other gods and participating in other religions. God said, "You're committing adultery against Me, and I will not tolerate that kind of behavior."

Hosea's book is a classic study in *eschatology,* which is "the branch of theology concerned with final events, as death." It is also a divine warning, a clarion call to take immediate corrective action.

Hosea describes three instruments used to sound the loud alarms God was utilizing to shake the hearts of His people. He first says to "blow the horn, or cornet, in Gibeah." *Cornet* means "the shofar" in Hebrew, an instrument made from a ram's horn. The word *shofar* literally means "to be glistening clear" or "to be clean."

Next Hosea mentions the trumpet. He orders, "Sound the trumpet in Ramah." The word *trumpet* means, "to emit a resounding call" or "sundered or quavering waves of sound." In other words, the trumpet sent out a sound that quavered with waves. You've heard of sound waves—the further the waves go, the stronger they become.

First Corinthians 14:8 says, *Again, if the trumpet does not sound a clear call, who will get ready for battle?* All of the sounds listed in Hosea 5:8 are sounds of urgency and emergency. They are alarms announcing that something is very wrong—all is *not* well. You'd better rise up...show concern...prepare yourself—something is definitely up.

Warning sounds from America's shores

When I was in South Africa in the late '90s, alarming sounds from America were being heard on the shores of a distant land.

Newspaper headlines where I was staying spoke of America's troubles with its president as well as bombings in Afghanistan and Sudan.

Soon after we left South Africa, a terrorist bomb went off in Capetown, not far from where we had been. When I read about the alarms that were going off—prophetic signals in that hour—I began to notice that what takes place in the natural is a sign of what is happening in the supernatural.

These terrorists were making sounds. The root word *terror* means "to strike fear in the heart of mankind." Little did we know then that terrorism would come to America's own shores in September 2001 and strike fear in the hearts of mankind.

Terrorists who had never affiliated with one another before were meeting together for the express purpose of destroying the United States of America—the only country in the world whose currency reads, "In God We Trust."

I saw in the spirit realm that principalities, powers, and rulers of darkness were assembling and allying themselves for the final episode of God's eternal plan. They were determined to destroy the people of God—to strike terror and fear in the greatest city on the Atlantic seaboard—amazingly close in proximity to where America's original settlers had landed after crossing the ocean to escape fear, frustration, exploitation, and religious persecution.

> I SAW IN THE SPIRIT REALM THAT PRINCIPALITIES, POWERS, AND RULERS OF DARKNESS WERE ASSEMBLING AND ALLYING THEMSELVES FOR THE FINAL EPISODE OF GOD'S ETERNAL PLAN. THEY WERE DETERMINED TO DESTROY THE PEOPLE OF GOD...

Now the princes of darkness were formulating plans to strike at the very areas in which Americans had always felt secure. These fateful events sounded an urgent warning—alarms—prophetic signals that the end was near.

Instead of heeding the warning signs (sounds), Americans complacently focused their attention on Senate and Congressional hearings to determine the definition of *sex* and *sex education.*

We would awaken from our smug, self-satisfying sleep on Tuesday, September 11, 2001—a date *People* magazine called "The Day That Shook America"—to learn that life as we had known it would be forever altered by rogue terrorist organizations called Al-Qaida and the Taliban. More importantly, we would come to realize that there had been warnings about these groups for many years, but we weren't paying attention.

Blessed are they who know the joyful sound!

Hosea also talks about the sound of the battle cry. The term used literally means, "to split the ears with volume." Psalm 89:15 KJV says, *Blessed is the people that know the joyful sound: they shall walk, O Lord, in the light of thy countenance.* The Hebrew word translated *joyful sound* is the same word used in Hosea for "the battle cry." Blessed are the people who recognize and respond appropriately to the battle cry.

WE DON'T HAVE TIME TO BE FOOLING AROUND AND FULFILLING THE LUST OF THE FLESH WHILE THERE'S A WAR GOING ON IN THE SPIRIT REALM.

The sounds of prophecy were going off all around us in the late nineties and at the turn of the millennium. I don't know if you heard it like I heard it, but I recognized the news reports coming from the White House, the schoolhouse, and the church house to be warnings and alarms sounding. They were prophetic sounds rallying this generation, saying, "Get ready. Prepare your weapons. Beat your pruning hooks into swords. It is time for war."

There's a battle cry sounding today against the unprecedented violence we're witnessing among children. Seven- and eight-year-old boys are *raping* seven- and eight-year-old girls. It doesn't make sense.

While America's elected officials' attention was turned to determining whether or not our former president's acts were impeachable offenses, the plan for a terrorist attack on American soil was underway. We don't need a prophetic anointing to understand that a warning is being sounded in this last day, declaring that we don't have time to be fooling around and fulfilling the lust of the flesh while there's a war going on in the spirit realm. We *must* pay attention!

Prophecy doesn't only operate in sound bytes

Prophecy does not only operate in the realm of sounds. It also operates in designated places. When Hosea prophesied specifically about geographical locations, he was recalling something from the past that must be remembered and reestablished for the future.

He specifically named three places of prophecy: Gibeah, Ramah, and Beth-aven. These are the places where the sounds are taking place. *Gibeah* means "the hill." It is a city in the territory occupied by the tribe of Benjamin, lying north of Jerusalem, and the birthplace of King Saul. It is where the Benjamites originally backslid.

Gibeah is where the Benjamites refused to hand over the men of Gibeah and their fellow tribesmen raped the Levite's concubine all night long and left her, battered and near death, at the threshold of the home where she and her master were visiting. This outrageous act resulted in civil war and the near-extinction of Benjamin (see Judges 19).

Gibeah is where Saul built his palace, and it is also the location where the backslidden king hid in fear from the Philistine army, while his son Jonathan and Jonathan's armor-bearer attacked Israel's enemy (see 1 Samuel 13-15).

This is the place where Samuel arrived and told Saul that the kingdom of God had been torn away from him. So Gibeah is the area that represents backsliding.

Gibeah is the root for the words found in Genesis 44, "the silver cup."

> *Now Joseph gave these instructions to the steward of his house: "Fill the men's sacks with as much food as they can carry, and put each man's silver in the mouth of his sack. Then put my cup, the silver one, in the mouth of the youngest one's sack, along with the silver for his grain." And he did as Joseph said.*
>
> —Genesis 44:1,2

Pharaoh had given Joseph the cup of his authority. When Joseph's brothers went to get their father in order to reconcile the entire family, Joseph had his own silver cup placed in Benjamin's sack. Why? To set up a confrontation to deal with the old issue of brother abandonment. This ploy set the stage for the moment of truth. The silver cup in Benjamin's sack would put the little brother's life in danger. Joseph wanted to see if the brothers who had sold him years before would ruthlessly abandon another brother. *Gibeah is the place where responsibility is neglected.*

Ramah means "the elevated place" or "the seat of idolatry." It was a city of Benjamin, situated between Gaba and Bethel. Samuel was born in Ramah. He lived there all his life, died there, and was buried there. Jeremiah 31 tells us that Ramah is the place where Rachel, Benjamin's mother, was buried.

Jeremiah 31:15 says, … *"A voice is heard in Ramah, mourning and great weeping, Rachel weeping for her children and refusing to be comforted, because her children are no more."*

Gibeah and Ramah are symbolically crucial to the last-day unveiling of God's plan. These two places represent the line of separation where God's people are divided. They sit in the confines of two kingdoms—Judah and Israel—that were supposed to be one. One city represents Samuel, the prophet, and the other represents Saul, the king.

The spirit of arrogance

Last, Hosea said to "sound the battle cry in Beth-aven." *Beth-aven* means "the house of vanity." Beth-aven was originally referred to as Bethel. Bible students understand that *Bethel* means "the house of God." The house of God had been degenerated to the house of deception, vanity, and nothingness. It had become a place of pride, conceit, and arrogance with only the appearance of accomplishment and success.

> THE HOUSE OF GOD HAD BEEN DEGENERATED TO THE HOUSE OF DECEPTION, VANITY, AND NOTHINGNESS.

It's amazing what position can do to people in the house of God. People who were once the epitome of humble servanthood suddenly become arrogant and prideful when they're given a title and position. Those who used to want to serve people suddenly feel as though they have "arrived" and have the right to be abrupt and rude because of their lofty position. Position and title have changed them. Their lives used to stand for something—now they stand for nothing.

Jesus said, … *"My house will be called a house of prayer, but you are making it a 'den of robbers'"* (Matthew 21:13). I call it the degeneration of God's house.

We are the generation referred to in 2 Timothy 3:1-5:

> *But mark this: There will be terrible times in the last days. People will be lovers of themselves, lovers of money,*

boastful, proud, abusive, disobedient to their parents, ungrateful, unholy, without love, unforgiving, slanderous, without self-control, brutal, not lovers of the good, treacherous, rash, conceited, lovers of pleasure rather than lovers of God—having a form of godliness but denying its power....

We used to enter the house of God and actually feel the fire of the Holy Ghost and the power of the anointing. Today we have become no more than spiritually destitute "groupies" assembling to pay empty homage to a personality. There's no power in the pulpit and no praise in the pew. It's just a house of vanity. We're in a mess. *Watch out, Benjamin.*

God has a people for every problem

TOMORROW'S GENERATION IS NOT GOING TO ACCOMPLISH WHAT OUR GENERATION WAS CALLED TO DO. YESTERDAY'S GENERATION COULD NOT FIT THIS TIME WE'RE LIVING IN. THIS IS OUR TERRITORY.

In our Hosea text, God does not call for Judah when he sees the mess that is going on in Gibeah, Ramah, and Beth-aven. He does not call for Joseph or Levi, but for Benjamin. Why would the Lord call for Benjamin instead of someone else? It was Benjamin's territory.

Tomorrow's generation is not going to accomplish what our generation was called to do. Yesterday's generation could not fit this time we're living in. This is our territory. Gibeah belongs to us. Ramah belongs to us. Beth-aven belongs to us.

It's a God thing!

In crying out for a deliverer from this ungodly mess, Hosea screams, "Benjamin, come forth! Benjamin, lead on!" He called for Benjamin because only Benjamin understood Gibeah—it was his territory! It was his homeland. *That mess belonged to him!* There's a battle cry going on in the silver cup of Benjamin's authority. Joseph placed the silver cup in Benjamin's sack because he knew Benjamin would be the instrument God would use to bring the whole family back together.

There's a cup in your sack, Benjamite, and God is crying out, "Bring the races together—blacks, whites, Hispanics, and Orientals—and return to Me. This is a generation of reconciliation. I've put My silver cup in your sack. I'm holding you responsible for this generation."

Don't let the words *segregation* and *division* touch you. When you hear the word *segregation,* remember what you've got in your sack. There's a silver cup that says you are responsible for bringing God's family together. It's not a black thing, a white thing, a Hispanic thing, or an Oriental thing. It's a God thing!

No one knows how to deal with the "Gibeahs" of life like you do. No one knows how to deal with "Ramah" like a Benjamite. If this generation wants reconciliation, call Benjamin.

The spirit of prophecy lives in us, and Benjamin must go back to Ramah and say, "Where the prophet died, we will resurrect the spirit of prophecy and call things that are not as though they are."

We will look at a future of chaos and say, "Come to order, every piece of you. My family, my finances, and my future must align itself with the Word of God." That's the spirit of prophecy.

The Benjamin blessing is on you to anoint, impart, and place the mantle of holiness on your generation and the next if Jesus tarries. The spirit of prophecy has died and must be resurrected. Now is the time for men to look at their sons and daughters and say, "You're going to be a man (woman) of God. I don't care what society says. I don't care what statistics say."

A spirit of resistance fights the Benjamin blessing

I love a good fight. I love it when the devil comes against a word from God. I've never seen God's Word lose. There's a spirit of resistance fighting the Benjamin blessing that tells me that something is about to happen. Anytime you start preaching a prophetic word...anytime you start addressing a right-now situation in the church...the devil doesn't like it.

I dare you to get out your checkbook right now and prophesy to it, saying, "You shall live and not die." Look at your children and say, "You're going to be obedient if it's the last thing I do." Prophesy to your spouse, your children, your friends, and your neighbors. Say to them, "You're not going to worry yourself to death. You're not going to have to starve yourself to get my attention. You're not going to have to take mind-numbing drugs to help you go through a depressing adolescence. You're not going to be an alcoholic or a racist. You're not going to be small-minded and full of prejudice. No, you're going to be a man or woman of God."

Prophesy! Benjamin, stand up and speak out. This world's in a mess, looking for believers who are not self-centered, selfish, and prejudiced, but who know how to walk prophetically in God's Word.

Nobody but Benjamin knew how to deal with a church that used to possess glory but had become a house of nothing but vanity. So Hosea says, "In Beth-aven, sound the battle cry. Get Benjamin in there."

God knows how to operate with nothing

Do you know why you were born for this generation? Because God knew this generation would be an X generation—a generation of nothingness, vain, self-serving, indulged, and indulgent.

God has anointed you with the Benjamin blessing to exchange your nothing for something significant. In churches where nothing is happening, Benjamites are rising up and making something happen. In jobs where nothing is happening, Benjamites are leading and making something happen.

God knows how to operate with nothing. In fact, He does His best work when He starts with nothing. If your marriage is nothing, let God get hold of it. If your family is nothing, let God get hold of it. If your job is nothing, let God get hold of it. If your ministry is nothing, let God get hold of it. If your life feels like it's nothing, get a Benjamite spirit down on the inside of you and say, "Something is coming out of my nothing...starting right now!"

> GOD HAS ANOINTED YOU WITH THE BENJAMIN BLESSING TO EXCHANGE YOUR NOTHING FOR SOMETHING SIGNIFICANT.

The spirit of the lover is hovering over you!

Genesis 1:1 says the Spirit of the Lord hovered over the face of the deep, formless and void, no order...nothing. And God said, "Let there be light," and there was light (v.3). Something came out of nothing.

I look at Family Praise Center—the church in San Antonio, Texas, where I pastor—and realize that when we started several years ago, we were $20,000 in debt. That's sub-nothing—that's below nothing. I drove up one Sunday morning recently, looked around at all the buildings and said, "Something!"

Every now and then I look at my life and say, "I was nothing, but God made me something." Benjamites have an attitude that demands something good to come out of nothing.

If you want revelation, you're going to have to go against the tide. The Benjamite spirit says, "Listen, I don't follow tradition. I'm not bound by the way we've always done it. I believe God is saying, *Remember ye not the former things, neither consider the things of old. Behold, I will do a new thing; now it shall spring forth; shall ye not know it? I will even make a way in the wilderness, and rivers in the desert* (Isaiah 43:18,19 KJV).

The Benjamite anointing is coming to your house!

There is a Benjamite anointing coming on the house of God in this last day. It is so radical that the people of God are going to come eager to enter into praise. The people will be so hungry for praise that they'll come, saying, "I don't need a singer or an instrument. I've got so much to praise my God about that I'm about to explode!"

Like Israel in Hosea's time, the twenty-first century bride of Christ has been unfaithful to her bridegroom. We've chased after fame, recognition, and personal prosperity. We've focused on the meaningless and empty accumulation of material wealth. Some of our finest leaders have succumbed to lusts of the flesh and caused the house of God to become a literal den of robbers. The church has lowered its standard until it is so similar to the world around it that even an astute observer can't discern the difference between the two.

Hosea 5:8 AMP says: *Blow the horn in Gibeah and the trumpet in Ramah [both lofty hills on Benjamin's northern border]. Sound the alarm at Beth-aven: [the enemy is] behind you and after you, O Benjamin [be on your guard]!*

The enemy's not only behind you, but he intends to take you out. Know this: if he's behind you, that means you're in front of him. If he has to try to catch you, then you're already outdoing him.

The Benjamite spirit says, "Run, devil, run, and you'd better have some good Nikes if you're going to catch me. I'm blazing a trail of glory and leaving you in my dust. If you should catch me, you'll be sorry you ever got close to me, because I'm going to come against you with something you've never seen or felt."

> *Be well balanced (temperate, sober of mind), be vig-*
> *ilant and cautious at all times; for that enemy of yours,*
> *the devil, roams around like a lion roaring [in fierce*
> *hunger], seeking someone to seize upon and devour.*
> —1 Peter 5:8 AMP

You don't have to run. The Philistine champion, Goliath, shouted at David, the shepherd boy who would be Israel's king, "Come here, and I'll give your flesh to the birds of the air and the beasts of the field!" David answered, "No, you won't be doing that today. I will give the carcasses of the Philistine army to the birds of the air and the beasts of the earth, and the whole world will know that there is a God in Israel" (see 1 Samuel 17:44-46 paraphrased).

The Benjamite generation is calling for people who will stand up and say, "I'm not Generation Nothing. I'm Generation Something. I have a part to play in this final hour of the church of Jesus Christ, when one generation passes the anointing on to another generation. We know how to deal with Ramah, Gibeah, and Beth-aven."

> THE BENJAMITE GENERATION IS CALLING FOR PEOPLE WHO WILL STAND UP AND SAY, "I'M NOT GENERATION NOTHING. I'M GENERATION SOMETHING..."

God wants to deal with your nothingness right now. He can take a life that is nothing and make it something. He can bring order to your chaos. God can fill the void of your heart. When everything around you is falling down, it's time for you to stand up, Benjamin. Your time of blessing has come.

Take your place. Open your life and your heart to the power of God. Jesus has come to fill the void. Invite Him to come in. You are blessed to become a blessing!

9

The Benjamin Church

As he looked about and saw his brother Benjamin, his own mother's son, he asked, "Is this your youngest brother, the one you told me about?" And he said, "God be gracious to you, my son." Deeply moved at the sight of his brother, Joseph hurried out and looked for a place to weep...and wept there. After he had washed his face, he came out and, controlling himself, said, "Serve the food."

The men had been seated before him in the order of their ages, from the firstborn to the youngest.... When portions were served to them from Joseph's table, Benjamin's portion was five times as much as anyone else's....

To each of them he gave new clothing, but to Benjamin he gave three hundred shekels of silver and five sets of clothes.

—Genesis 43:29-31,33,34; 45:22

What is a *Benjamin* church?

It is not a building with pews inside and a billboard on the freeway. It is a worldwide spiritual union of members of the body of Christ who recognize their purpose and act in a *Benjamin*-like way to fulfill their calling. It is the seventh-millennium, radical church filled with radical people. Benjamites are ever seeking and pursuing, with praise in their mouths and purpose in their hearts.

The Benjamin Church is magnetic. People are drawn to wherever Benjamites come together—a place sure to be filled with prayer and praise. As Benjamites, we are excited about our salvation, demonstrate a passion for our Savior, and have an overwhelming love for our Father in heaven. Our ignited passion serves as a beacon of hope, drawing people from all levels of society. We—you and I—are God's answer to the needs of hopeless humanity in these last days.

YOU AND I ARE GOD'S ANSWER TO THE NEEDS OF HOPELESS HUMANITY IN THESE LAST DAYS.

Benjamin-blessed believers have been imparted with a bold militancy that tears down many preconceived ideas about the church's purpose. We break through traditional ethnic, economic, and educational barriers and march forward to rescue and gather the end-time harvest.

We are not an exclusive club—we welcome the oppressed, the downtrodden, those who have been discriminated against, and those who, by no choice of their own, were born into hopelessness, lack, and a sense of helplessness. The Benjamin Church actively seeks to help every individual fulfill his purpose and destiny.

The tribe of Benjamin was filled with great hope and, at times, great failure, dynamic adventure, fierce battles, and remarkable blessings. Its help came from the most unlikely places at the most unlikely times. To the Benjamite today there is a meaning for every moment, a purpose for every hour, a destiny for every day, and a prophetic vision for every tomorrow.

From the beginning, Benjamin's life illustrated individuality and a peculiar, singular path that many of us can relate to today. He was raised in a single-parent household as a result of his mother's death immediately following his birth. This situation brought about a close relationship with Jacob, his father.

Fatherless Christianity: a curse on the church

A few years ago, Attorney General John D. Ashcroft wrote a

wonderful tribute to his beloved father in a book entitled, *Lessons From a Father to His Son.* He said, "On the eve of my induction into the U.S. Senate, I asked a small group of family and friends to pray for me. As they circled around me, I noticed my father beginning to rise from the couch, "That's okay, Dad," I said. "You don't have to stand up to pray for me."

"I'm not struggling to stand," his father replied. "I'm struggling to kneel."

"I saw this as a defining moment of my life," Ashcroft writes, "I thought, *What would this country and the Christian church be like if more fathers struggled to kneel on behalf of their children?*"

A strong father influence pervades both naturally and spiritually in the Benjamin Church. Just as a good father is diligent in fulfilling his responsibilities to his family, while maintaining his personal relationship with his heavenly Father, so the Benjamin Church radiates with the influence of Father God. This strong relationship with the Father will dramatically alter the dynamic of our society, helping to fulfill the prophetic words of Malachi with regard to the last-day church:

> *"He will turn the hearts of the fathers to their children, and the hearts of the children to their fathers; or else I will come and strike the land with a curse."*
> —Malachi 4:6

The dying Rachel had called her son *Ben-oni,* or "son of my sorrow." As much as Jacob loved Rachel, just before she breathed her last breath, he stepped forward and renounced that curse. "This boy will *not* be called a son of sorrow," Jacob said, "but he will be called *Benjamin,* which means the 'son of my right hand.'" The right hand represents a position of authority, and is mentioned in that context 160 times in Scripture.

Hebrews 12:2 says when Jesus sat down at the *right hand* of the throne of God, He was given authority by virtue of His position. With his father's name change, Benjamin was transformed in a moment of time from a son of sorrow to a son of authority.

WITH HIS FATHER'S NAME CHANGE, BENJAMIN WAS TRANSFORMED IN A MOMENT OF TIME FROM A SON OF SORROW TO A SON OF AUTHORITY.

That same transformation is desperately needed in the latter day church. I asked the Lord why the church has lost its position and so much of its authority, and I felt impressed to review the story of the prodigal son in Luke 15.

Have you ever had lunch with a pig?

This young man had asked his father for his inheritance and *...set off for a distant country and there squandered his wealth in wild living* (Luke 15:13). He quickly wasted the fruits of his father's abundance to the point that he jumped into a pigpen and wrestled the hogs for food to silence the groaning of his starving belly!

But the prodigal learned something about himself in the pigpen. He'd lost something on which no monetary value could be set—his relationship with his father. He never mentioned his mother, but verses 17-20 say, *"When he came to his senses, he said, 'How many of my father's hired men have food to spare, and here I am starving to death! I will set out and go back to my father and say to him: Father, I have sinned against heaven and against you. I am no longer worthy to be called your son; make me like one of your hired men.' So he got up and went to his father."*

The prodigal chose to change. He knew exactly where to go when he was at the end of his rope—he needed to return to his father. When he came to his senses, he realized that he'd rather be a slave in his father's house than to be out from under his father's covering. But when he returned, the young man's dad was waiting on him. He put a ring on his finger, a robe on his back, sandals on his feet, and threw the biggest party that county had ever seen!

God is waiting for us to come home

The Lord helped me see that He is waiting for us to come back to Him. He is still our Father. The mother has called us a sorrowful people. The church has called us negative names, implying that we've caused much pain—and sadly, it's true. But God says, "I will transform men and women in this hour who have left positions of authority to wallow with pigs, and I won't leave the porch until they return to their rightful position. I have given them a place of authority, and it's at My right hand."

Benjamite, you are not a fatherless orphan! You are a child of God's right hand, called to be a "son of authority." The position that has been lost will be restored to the Benjamin Church. In this last hour, the devil will tell you that you lost it, never had it, or you'll never get it back. That's when you can challenge Satan's taunts with a profound statement of fact.

> YOU ARE A CHILD OF GOD'S RIGHT HAND, CALLED TO BE A "SON OF AUTHORITY."

Now, maybe you aren't in the habit of squaring off with the devil. But, I want you to know that you can win every confrontation by saturating your atmosphere with this attitude: "Satan, I know who I am. My name is Benjamin. I am not a son of sorrow but a son of authority. My Father says so. Now, hit the trail and don't come around here again!"

The body of Christ has a problem with headship. In 2 Kings 6, a group of prophets decided to go over to Jordan and build a school. After making this decision, they informed their teacher, Elisha, and he wasn't happy with the idea. He knew that they were called to be prophets—not carpenters. When they chopped down a tree and lost the ax head, they had to call for help. The man of God came and asked, "Where did you lose your head?" (my paraphrase).

That is the problem in the body of Christ today. For too long, pastors and fathers have been doing what the flock (children) want instead of exerting leadership. The kingdom of God is not a democracy. It is not for the people to decide when it's time to transition. Where did God's chosen leaders lose their spiritual authority? Where did we as a church lose our spiritual fathers? Where did you lose the men of God who speak into your life and impact you so that you respect and reverence God and His Word?

The fatherless generation

There are a lot of people around who can't wait to tell you what you've done wrong, but there aren't many fathers willing to take the time and effort to help you grow up.

—1 Corinthians 4:15 The Message

ONE CAN RECEIVE INFORMATION AT ANY OLD CONFERENCE, BUT HE WILL ONLY RECEIVE IMPARTATION FROM THE MAN WHO IS FATHERING HIM.

We live in a fatherless generation where fathers have walked out on their kids right in the middle of their adolescent years—walked away from them. Why? It's easier to selfishly focus on the age-old "What about me?" question than it is to willingly sacrifice all that you have and all that you are for your kids. The result: many young people have joined gangs in order to experience a sense of family. They even wear "colors" to identify themselves as members of something bigger than themselves. But the spirit of the father is coming back to the body of Christ, and young men will listen to older men and older men will be patient with younger men. Being a father requires commitment.

The Benjamin Church is about to receive a revelation about family. One can receive information at any old conference, but he will only receive impartation from the man who is fathering him.

I agree with California pastor, Bayless Conley. His book, *The Miracle of Mentoring, A Biblical Guide to Spiritual Fathering,* says, "Spiritual fathers sow seeds just as natural fathers do! If your wife gets pregnant, you are not going to wonder how it happened. You know how it happened! To expect people to be saved (birthed spiritually) without planting the seed of the Word in their hearts is like a husband and wife praying for a baby and never sharing sexual intimacy! Human beings can only become natural parents through the act of planting seeds. And we can only become spiritual parents through the act of planting incorruptible seeds." Webster defines *incorruptible* as "honest; incapable of ruining or undermining the integrity of."

Pastor Conley goes on to say something very important, "Seeds are no respecter of persons. They will grow for me just as they will grow for the career farmer." Plant some good seeds, Benjamin.

A father prays over his children—sometimes in agonizing travail. They are always *with* him, whether or not they're miles apart. I have a friend who is the father of three beautiful little girls. Jake's ministry involves a great deal of travel, and he misses his wife and his girls when he's away from home. Many times I've heard him say, "I can close my eyes and *smell* my babies." They may not be within a thousand miles of each other, but those babies are *with* him all the time.

Elisha did not cry, "My mentor, my mentor," when Elijah was taken up by the chariots of fire (see 2 Kings 2:11,12). You don't get a mantle from mentors—only a father can put his mantle on you. Impartation comes from men of God who discipline, instruct, and stay with you week in and week out. I prophesy that that's why there are prophets and apostles who will be born into the Benjamin generation in the last day who will know who they are and be secure in their position in the family of God. They will not compromise. They will not back down. And they will preach an undefiled, undiluted, unpolluted message of Jesus Christ.

Satan may trip you, but he won't trap you!

GOD KNOWS WHAT IT WILL TAKE FOR US TO GET THROUGH THESE CHALLENGING TIMES, SO, LIKE BENJAMIN OF OLD, GOD IS GOING TO GIVE US FIVE TIMES THE PROVISION OF ANY GENERATION THAT HAS GONE BEFORE US.

The last-day church will not survive on yesterday's experience. God knows what it will take for us to get through these challenging times, so, like Benjamin of old, God is going to give us five times the provision of any generation that has gone before us.

For the Lord has chosen Zion, he has desired it for his dwelling: "This is my resting place for ever and ever; here I will sit enthroned, for I have desired it—I will bless her with abundant provisions; her poor will I satisfy with food. I will clothe her priests with salvation, and her saints will ever sing for joy.

—Psalm 132:13-16

Those backslidden failures you've given up on are going to come bouncing back because God has said in His Word that He has clothed them with salvation! They can run, but they cannot hide. They can change course, but the clothes (of salvation) will never change.

But allow me to warn you, Benjamite! Do not let your insatiable, ravenous appetite lead you back into the world. Stay on guard! Unbridled passion can lead to sensuous activity. A problem with the Benjamin church is perception—a certain difficulty in distinguishing between sensuality and sensitivity. The definition of *sensual* refers to "being preoccupied with the gratification of physical appetites—not spiritual or intellectual, but physical or worldly."

Sensitive, on the other hand, is defined as "capable of perceiving with a sense or senses; responsive to external conditions; susceptible to the ideas, emotions, or circumstances of others." So passion can be a problem to the Benjamite.

We can easily become discontented when our passions aren't stirred, or when we're not in perpetual motion. We have a tendency to settle during these "down" times and become listless, bored, and idle...until the next emotional outburst comes along. Emotions are fickle! They cannot be trusted! That's when we need to go some place and get quiet and, as recorded in Psalm 46:10, *"Be still, and know that I am God; I will be exalted among the nations, I will be exalted in the earth."*

We can be very sensually driven people. That's why we make celebrities out of preachers, and this ought not to be. That's a *concert* mentality—not a *conference* mentality. We celebrate the individual, which makes us personality driven, not presence driven. Why? We're more interested in the *messenger* than the *message*.

Sadly, we seem to try to be as much like the world as we can be, instead of celebrating our uniqueness. Benjamin, our message is different from the world's! Please get this. Our standards are different. Our morals are different. Our values are different. Our purpose is different. While the world—and unfortunately, much of the modern day church—is totally given over to the sensual, we should be living in the Spirit.

Benjamites recognize that we are not earthly beings having a spiritual experience, but we are spiritual beings having an earthly experience!

BENJAMITES RECOGNIZE THAT WE ARE NOT EARTHLY BEINGS HAVING A SPIRITUAL EXPERIENCE, BUT WE ARE SPIRITUAL BEINGS HAVING AN EARTHLY EXPERIENCE!

"But he who has been forgiven little loves little" (Luke 7:47). There is a hidden danger residing in those of us who have been rescued by the power of His Spirit. When you've been through some things, there's a craving that must be crucified daily. The Bible says we are driven...we are wolves ...we are hungry, but we must satisfy our appetite with the worship of the Lord God Almighty.

We're not finished building testimonies. God not only delivered me from drugs when I was 14 years old, but He also delivers me daily from the trials and tribulations that I go through right now. God is establishing a testimony in me so I can overcome the enemy by the blood of the Lamb and the word of my testimony (see Revelation 12:11). You might see a Benjamite trip, but you won't see him trapped.

God's got you covered!

It was customary in ancient times that when serving a banquet where a king was present, the king was given a double portion of food, or twice the serving of any other guest. Joseph, however, served his brother Benjamin *five times more* food than any of his half brothers. Then he gave Benjamin *five changes* of clothing! What about this five-fold blessing?

Five is the number of grace. When Moses, who could be considered a father to the tribes of Israel because of his role as leader, pronounced his blessing on all the tribes just before his death, *About*

Benjamin he said: *"Let the beloved of the Lord rest secure in him, for he shields him all day long, and the one the Lord loves rests between his shoulders"* (Deuteronomy 33:12). That's grace! As a Benjamite, you're covered!

One definition of the word *cover* refers to "placing something on or over, so as to protect; to wrap up: clothe; to protect, as from enemy attack." *Changes* means "an alteration; to change course." *Raiment* as used in the King James Version of Genesis 45:22 means "to cover; a mantle that assumes the shape of the object that is covered." From this, I believe the Benjamin Church will abound in provision and be blessed with five times the ability to change and be favored with five times the covering or protection. God has you covered!

When you join the Benjamin Church, God cloaks you with five *changes* of clothes so that you can adapt to any environment in which you find yourself. You have more than one chance...more than two chances. God is saying, "You will have the ability to wear more than one hat—to adapt or alter your life as necessary to be able to succeed in any assignment because I'll give you enough grace for every season of your life."

> GOD WILL NEVER GIVE UP ON THOSE WHO RIGHTFULLY CLAIM THE BENJAMIN BLESSING. HE'LL GIVE US NOT ONE CHANCE, NOT TWO CHANCES...NOT EVEN THREE OR FOUR...BUT *FIVE* TIMES THE OPPORTUNITIES TO ALTER OUR COURSE IF WE GET OFF-TRACK.

God will never give up on those who rightfully claim the Benjamin blessing. He'll give us not one chance, not two chances ...not even three or four...but *five* times the opportunities to alter our course if we get off-track. We are no longer children of sorrow but children of authority.

A remnant Benjamite of Israel

In Paul's letter to the church in Rome, he asked: *Did God reject his people? By no means! I am an Israelite myself, a descendant of Abraham, from the tribe of Benjamin. God did not reject his people, whom he foreknew...At the present time there is a remnant chosen by grace* (Romans 11:1,2,5).

At Philippi, Paul declared, *...If anyone else thinks he has reasons to put confidence in the flesh, I have more: circumcised on the eighth day, of the people of Israel, of the tribe of Benjamin, a Hebrew of Hebrews; in regard to the law, a Pharisee; as for zeal, persecuting the church; as for legalistic righteousness, faultless* (Philippians 3:4-6).

In common terms, Paul was saying, "I'm not ashamed to tell you that I've messed up. I've made some big mistakes. People have counted me out, but I belong to the tribe of Benjamin. Before you give up on me, let me remind you of where I came from. I came from a mountain of testimonies. I know who I am. My membership is in the Benjamin Church. Follow me, and I'll lead you to Christ, the King of kings and Lord of lords!"

Paul taught his listeners to see in Jesus a man like themselves who was at the same time uniquely the Son of God, prepared to share with them His kinship with the Father. Religion then became a deeply personal experience, no longer a matter of fate, duty, or fear but a doctrine of personal grace and love addressed to all men. Moreover, it was not centered in a temple or shrine but in men's hearts.

He believed that the gospel, crucifixion, and resurrection of Jesus signified a new covenant with the Lord, complementing the old covenant. He was convinced that Jeremiah the prophet had foreseen this: *"No longer will a man teach his neighbor, or a man his brother, saying, 'Know the Lord,' because they will all know me, from the least of them to the greatest,"* declares the Lord. *"For I will forgive their wickedness and will remember their sins no more"* (Jeremiah 31:34).

Paul's message wasn't universally accepted. The authorities threw him in jail numerous times, beat him up, and threatened heinous acts against him. His reaction went something like this: "I belong to the tribe of Benjamin. You can put me behind bars and tell me I'm busted. You can try to shut me down, lock me up, cut off my head, boil me in oil—and if that doesn't work, crucify me upside down—but this is what will happen.

"I'll write two-thirds of the New Testament. I will establish a vital network of Christian churches and an extensive Christian theology with my letters, conveying the full richness of my personal experience with Christ. I have the blood of Benjamin flowing through my veins. I'm a ravenous wolf in pursuit of God. You cannot stop me."

"Lord, what do we do?"

I prayed for God to give me some wonderful approach and presentation of His gospel in this last hour that would reach transgenerational groups. I asked Him to let it satisfy the old while reaching the young. God let me know that if I would exhibit His love for me, He would bring children to me. The Bible says, ...*I, if I be lifted up...will draw all men unto* me (John 12:32 KJV).

For years and years the church has frustrated itself knocking on doors, with minimal results. God caused me to know that when we have magnetic praise in His House and demonstrate an undying affection for our Savior, people will come. We don't have to invite people to a house fire. When a house is on fire, folks know it. They'll come to see what's burning.

In other words, when we Benjamites get God going in the sanctuary and unsaved folks come in, they'll enter His courts of praise with a hunger and thirst for what we have. They'll begin to realize that their lives aren't very exciting compared to ours.

The Benjamin Church will never allow anything to inhibit our praise. We praise God even in the midst of great trial and tribulation. Nothing we're going through can snuff out the praise in our hearts.

Come on, Benjamin, you're a ravenous wolf in pursuit of God. You have been given five times the blessings, five times the praise, five times the ability to change. You walk in grace. God will never leave you nor forsake you. You are the Benjamin Church! Go forth!

The Benjamin Creed

I am part of the Benjamin Church. The die has been cast. The decision has been made. I have stepped over the line. I won't look back, let up, slow down, back away, or be still. My past is redeemed. My present makes sense. My future is secure. I'm finished with low living, sight walking, small planning, smooth knees, colorless dreams, tamed visions, mundane talking, cheap giving, and dwarfed goals.

I am part of the Benjamin Church. I no longer need preeminence, position, promotion, or popularity. I don't have to be right, first, tops, recognized, praised, regarded, or rewarded. I now live by faith. I lean on His presence. I love with patience. I live by prayer. I labor with power.

I am part of the Benjamin Church. My face is set. My gait is fast. My goal is heaven. My road is narrow. My way is rough. My companions are few. My guide is reliable, and my mission is clear.

I am part of the Benjamin Church. I cannot be bought, compromised, detoured, lured away, turned back, deluded, or delayed. I will not flinch in the face of sacrifice, hesitate in the presence of adversity, negotiate at the table of the enemy, ponder at the pool of popularity, or meander in the maze of mediocrity.

I am part of the Benjamin Church. I won't give up, shut up, let up, or slow up until I have stayed up, stored up, prayed up, paid up, and spoken up for the cause of Christ.

I am part of the Benjamin Church. I must go until He comes, give until I drop, preach until all know, and work until He stops me. And when Jesus comes for His own, He will have no problem recognizing me, for my banner is clear. I am part of the Benjamin Church.

—Adapted by Rick Hawkins from the writings of a young African pastor prior to his martyrdom and published in *The Signature of Jesus* by Brennan Manning.

Prayer of Salvation

Lord, I thank You for this opportunity to come into relationship with You today. I confess with my mouth that You are Lord. I now make a conscious decision to turn away from a life of sin and to live for You. I will read my Bible. I will pray every day. I will attend church regularly.

God, I believe You gave Your only Son, Jesus, to die for my sins. I believe that He rose again. I thank You for the gift of salvation. I receive that gift today. I will not look back. This is the most important decision of my life. My life is now Yours. I will never be the same. In Jesus' name, amen.

References

Ashcroft, John D. *Lessons From a Father to His Son*. Nashville: Thomas Nelson Publishers, 1998.

Barker, William P. *Everyone in the Bible*. Westwood: Fleming H. Revell Company, 1966.

Conley, Bayless. *The Miracle of Mentoring—A Biblical Guide to Spiritual Fathering*. Harrison House, Inc., Tulsa, Oklahoma, 2001.

Eerdman's Handbook to the Bible. New York: Guideposts edition published by special arrangement with Wm. B. Eerdmans Publishing Co., 1973.

Farrar, John. *People & Places in the Bible*. Barbour Books, Westwood, New Jersey, 1987.

Jackson, J.B. *A Dictionary of the Proper Names of the Old and New Testament Scriptures, Being an Accurate and Literal Translation from the Original Tongues*. Loizeaux Brothers, Neptune, New Jersey, 1909.

James, Kay Coles. *Never Forget: The Riveting Story of One Woman's Journey from the Projects to the Corridors of Power*. Zondervan Publishing, Grand Rapids, Michigan, 1995.

Lockyer, Dr. Herbert. *All the Apostles of the Bible*. Grand Rapids: Zondervan Publishing House, 1972.

Manning, Brennan. *The Signature of Jesus.* Multnomah Publishers, Inc., Sisters, Oregon, 1992.

Meyer, Joyce. *Battlefield of the Mind: Winning the Battle in Your Mind.* Harrison House, Inc., Tulsa, Oklahoma, 1995.

The New Compact Bible Dictionary. Grand Rapids: Regency Reference Library, an imprint of Zondervan Publishing House, 1967.

Smalley, Gary A. and John T. Trent. *The Blessing.* New York: POCKET BOOKS, a division of Simon & Schuster, Inc., 1986.

James E. Strong. *Strong's Exhaustive Concordance of the Bible,* "Hebrew and Chaldee Dictionary," "Greek Dictionary of the New Testament." Nashville: Abingdon, 1890.

Webster's II New World College Dictionary, 3rd ed. New York: Simon & Schuster, Inc., 1996.

About the Author

Rick Hawkins is the founder and pastor of the Family Praise Center, an integrated, multicultural church located in San Antonio, Texas. Home to over 3,000 members, Family Praise Center is dedicated to reaching the lost and empowering the body of Christ.

Rick and his wife Robin also founded the School of Excellence in Education, one of the largest and fastest-growing charter schools in Texas, reaching more than 1,000 at-risk children and youth in the San Antonio area. Their successful faith-based outreach school program, The Nehemiah Institute, works with city and state agencies as a last alternative for troubled and incarcerated teens.

Rick is founder and councilmember of the *Knights of the Round Table*, a national pastor's and leader's forum established for relationship, integrity, and accountability.

Pastor Rick and Robin, his mate and best friend of 25 years, have three children, Dustin, Crystal, and Kendra.

Other books by Rick Hawkins

David's Mighty Men: A Study in Loyalty

The Power of Agreement